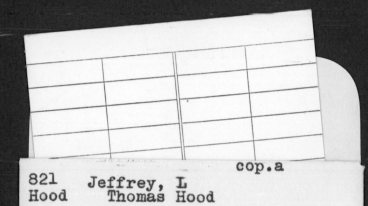

Twayne's English Authors Series 137

Sylvia E. Bowman, *Editor*

INDIANA UNIVERSITY

Thomas Hood

 **137**

Thomas Hood

By LLOYD N. JEFFREY

North Texas State University

Twayne Publishers, Inc.   ::   New York

Preface

The reputation of Thomas Hood, a literary figure very well known in England and America during his lifetime, is now pretty well summed up by the inscription on the Hood Memorial at Kensal Green: "HE SANG THE SONG OF THE SHIRT." Perusers of anthologies and students with a special interest in nineteenth-century poetry will recall also "The Bridge of Sighs," "I Remember, I Remember," and perhaps a few other pieces. Generally, however, Hood is not only overshadowed but eclipsed by the great Romantics who preceded and by the great Victorians who followed him. Hood deserves better, partly because of the intrinsic value of his work and partly because the study of his work leads us into an entire area of nineteenth-century literature that is usually neglected by all except the specialists.

One difficulty in studying Hood is the comparative unavailability of much of his work. The only complete edition of his poetry produced in this century, the Oxford Edition prepared by Walter Jerrold and published in 1906, has long been out of print. A good college library *might* have an edition of the Hood corpus edited by his children; but, with all due credit to this labor of love, it is poorly arranged, frequently erroneous, and sometimes even of questionable content since some selections are included as Hood's on speculative grounds. The *Memorials of Thomas Hood,* also prepared by the poet's son and daughter, has likewise serious deficiencies; it is, nevertheless, our major primary source for the facts of Hood's life and is hence invaluable.

Book-length studies of Hood, especially critical ones, are few indeed. Alexander Elliot's *Hood in Scotland* (1885) is of course limited in scope and is difficult to find. Walter Jerrold's *Thomas Hood: His Life and Times* (1907) remains a valuable book, although it is comparatively light on detailed criticism. Readers of Hood had to wait more than half a century for another full-length study: J. C. Reid's *Thomas Hood*, published in 1963, which is an excellent work; both sympathetic and judicious, it has doubtless done much to stimulate interest in its subject. This book differs from Reid's principally in that it devotes proportionately less space to the details of Hood's life and more to analyses of many separate works. (This remark is not meant to imply that Reid's study is *only* biographical, for it offers many fine critical insights.) Laurence Brander's *Thomas Hood*, a forty-seven-page survey that also appeared in 1963, is a useful introduction to the study of Hood. (Unfortunately, the author had no opportunity to use John Clubbe's *Victorian Forerunner: The Later Career of Thomas Hood* [1968], which appeared at about the time that this study was completed.) There are a good many articles and notes on Thomas Hood, some of them very helpful in the areas of their specific subjects; but many are concerned with minutiae or with personal appreciation rather than with criticism. Because the published criticism on Hood is, with the exceptions noted, spotty and inadequate, it has been cited in this study only in special cases.

This book traces the literary career of Thomas Hood from his first youthful attempts at verse to his emergence as a major humorist and finally to his role as a predominantly humanitarian poet during approximately the last year of his life. Separate chapters are devoted to the poetry reflecting Hood's fascination with the terrible and the grotesque and to his voluminous prose. The bulk of Hood's published work is so enormous as to necessitate a high degree of selectivity. Every effort has been made, therefore, to cover as many significant poems and prose pieces as possible without allowing the book to become crowded in appearance or superficial in treatment. The emphasis throughout is on Hood's writings, but biographical material is introduced when necessary for clarity and continuity. Some attention is given to the literary influences upon Hood and to his impact upon other writers; but the treatment of these and other scholarly matters is limited to suit the scope of a concise book intended for teachers, students, and general readers rather than for specialists. It is hoped that the study will prove a useful tool to readers who already have an interest in Hood and his period and that it will reveal to others the achievement of a man whose works have wit, charm, and often genuine artistic merit.

Acknowledgment is made to the Committee on Research, the

President, and the Board of Regents of North Texas State University for granting the author a leave of absence during the spring of 1968, without which the completion of this book would have been greatly delayed.

LLOYD N. JEFFREY

North Texas State University
Denton, Texas

Contents

Contents

Chronology

1799 Thomas Hood born May 23 in London, son of a bookseller and publisher of Scottish origin.

1811 Death of Hood's father forces change in educational plans.

1813 Hood forced to leave school to take position as clerk in London.

1814 Hood becomes interested in engraving through the influence of his uncle, a prominent engraver.

1815 Autumn, Hood has physical breakdown; journeys to Dundee to recover health and visit relatives.

1816 Still at Dundee, writes "The Bandit," a narrative poem somewhat in the vein of Sir Walter Scott and Lord Byron.

1817 Autumn, returns to London with the idea of following engraving as a profession.

1819– Hood working as an engraver. Makes occasional contribu-
1821 tions to a fortnightly literary society. Early summer, 1821, joins staff of the *London Magazine*. July, mother dies, leaving Hood's four sisters in his care.

1821– Working as "a sort of sub-editor" on the *London Magazine*.
1823 Meets Charles Lamb, J. H. Reynolds, Thomas De Quincey, William Hazlitt, William Wordsworth, and other prominent literary figures. Around June, 1823, severs association with the *London Magazine*.

1825 February, *Odes and Addresses to Great People,* by Hood and Reynolds, published with great success. May, marries Jane Reynolds.

1826 Publishes First Series of *Whims and Oddities,* which is very well received by the public and praised by *Blackwood's.* May (?)–August, employed as dramatic critic for *The Atlas.*

1827 February, publishes *National Tales,* a collection of stories, and in July, *The Plea of the Midsummer Fairies, Hero and Leander, Lycus the Centaur, and Other Poems*—both in the "serious tone," and both failures. October, Second Series of *Whims and Oddities* issued with great success.

1828 Writes a mediocre farce, *York and Lancaster or a School without Scholars* (one of several lackluster comedies attempted by Hood). October, begins editing *The Gem*, a "Christmas annual"; contributes to it "The Dream of Eugene Aram" and other pieces.

1829 Becomes one of the proprietors of *The Athenaeum*, a new and promising journal. September, scores a triumph with "The Epping Hunt."

1830 Hood brings out his first *Comic Annual* (to appear yearly 1830–39 and again in 1842), which is highly successful and widely imitated. Daughter, Frances, born.

1831 June, Hood unwisely ends his official connection with *The Athenaeum*, but continues to contribute to it.

1832 Moves with his family to a country house in Essex.

1833 Working on a three-volume novel, *Tylney Hall*. Harassed by poor health and heavy expenses.

1834 Hood quarrels with his publisher, C. Tilt; replaces him with A. H. Baily. October, *Tylney Hall* published and sells well, but Hood's finances still precarious. December, saddened by death of Lamb.

1835 Son, Tom, born. March, financial disaster sends Hood temporarily to the Continent. At Coblenz, plans a "German book"; continues work on *Comic Annual* and other projects.

1836 Supports Thomas Noon Talfourd's efforts toward reform of copyright law by writing for *The Athenaeum* a series of letters titled "Copyright and Copywrong." Winter, reveals increasing humanitarian concern with the poem "Agricultural Distress."

1837 June, moves with family to Ostend, Belgium. Continues work on *Comic Annual*. Autumn, planning *Hood's Own*, a monthly magazine.

1838 January, first issue of *Hood's Own* appears and wins instant popularity, but Hood's finances still critical. Returns to England for brief visit.

1839 Early in year, Hood in England briefly to consult Dr. Elliot about his health and to check into Baily's practices. Publishes the thirteen numbers of *Hood's Own* as a collected volume. December, publishes his "German book," *Up the Rhine* (dated 1840).

1840 *Up the Rhine* a phenomenal success, but Hood's income tied up through litigation with Baily. Summer, the Hood family finally reunited in England. November, Hood's *Athenaeum* review of Dickens' *Master Humphrey's Clock* leads to lasting friendship between the two writers. Scores a great hit with "Miss Kilmansegg and Her Precious Leg."

1841 Financial situation relieved somewhat by grant from Royal Literary Fund. August, Hood succeeds to editorship of the *New Monthly Magazine* upon death of Theodore Hook.

1842 Receives many marks of esteem from Dickens and other literary celebrities. June, publishes two more letters on copyright in *The Athenaeum*. Still editing the *New Monthly Magazine*.

1843 September, vacations with son in Dundee; visits Edinburgh and is entertained by Lord Jeffrey. October, quarrels with publisher of the *New Monthly Magazine* and resigns editorship. December, creates a sensation with "The Song of the Shirt"; publishes *Whimsicalities* (dated 1844).

1844 January, begins publication of *Hood's Monthly Magazine and Comic Miscellany;* sales are excellent, but again Hood has trouble with his publisher. Health collapses, and friends rally to keep the magazine on its feet. May, "The Bridge of Sighs" wins great acclaim. November, Mrs. Hood placed on civil pension list. Hood still trying to work while propped up in bed.

1845 May 3, Hood dies.

CHAPTER 1

Hood and the Romantic Age

THAT the Romantic age did not end with the death of Lord Byron nor even with the failure of Victor Hugo's *Les Burgraves* is now something of a commonplace; but the fact must be flatly stated to throw it against another commonplace, aging but tenacious: that Romanticism had the short, splendid life of a meteor that left its own rarefied atmosphere only to be destroyed through friction with a more substantial one. This paradox arises partly through a confusion of the apogee of Romanticism with its lasting but not always spectacular effects upon art and social consciousness. Although there was a tremendous *resurgence* of Romantic spirit around 1800, it is unnecessary to labor the point that Romanticism cannot be confined within chronological brackets; Robert Burns and Dylan Thomas were not the less Romantic for having completed their lives in the eighteenth and twentieth centuries, respectively.

Yet, knowing as we do that there were no funeral games for Dr. Samuel Johnson and no tutelary spirits at the birth of *Lyrical Ballads,* we are apt to slip into fuzzy generalizations about the demise of Romanticism and the rise of Victorianism. We do need to be reminded sometimes that nothing dramatic took place in literature with the accession of a naïve young princess and that, in fact, the "Victorian" ethos had its beginning before this event. But a more likely error than the one just glanced at is to see the two decades or so following the deaths of the great Younger Romantics as practically a complete interregnum. Granted that a void was left by the passing of Lord Byron, Percy Bysshe Shelley, and John Keats, we must realize that it was not total. A brilliant act is hard to follow, and the follower is apt to receive less than his due. Writers like Thomas Hood, Thomas Lovell Beddoes, George Darley, and John Clare deserve more than the negligent and super-

cilious treatment that is usually their lot in conventional surveys
of the Romantic period.

In a sense, the common idea that English Romanticism had
burned itself out by around 1825 or 1830 is, of course, correct. The
splendid young triumvirs were dead; the Older Romantics were, to
speak bluntly, simply older; certainly their increasing years had
brought no late spring. It could be contended, however, that, had
the Younger Romantics lived longer, they would have gone the
way of their elders—that the Romantic temper in England had
simply exhausted its store of psychic energy. This thesis, although
practically impossible to prove, is equally difficult to refute. The
"star-ypointing pyramid" stops its own course by reaching a point.
We do not find and have no right to expect a Keats or a Shelley
among Hood's contemporaries. Aside, however, from the per-
suasive argument that no human Icarus can long sustain his highest pitch (indeed, it is remarkable how sustained the Romantic
flight was), at least some of the causes for the change under examination must be sought in the shifting historical temper. Let us
acknowledge at once that the mutation was neither so sudden nor
so pronounced in character as is sometimes thought.

Hood's age was in its way as turbulent as Byron's and Shelley's,
an age of crisscrossing currents of traditionalism and experimenta-
tion in social and political attitudes as well as something of a
transitional era in the arts. The triumph of Saint George over the
Dragon at Waterloo created in England an atmosphere of "we-
showed-them" complacency accompanied by an almost panicky
fear of and intolerance toward any brand of revolutionary or even
liberal thought—this, too, when social conditions cried out for precisely this kind of thought and when, as in the hot noon of the
Romantic age, there were many who heeded the cry. For the most
part, though, these reformists of the 1830's and 1840's (and later)
leaned more toward pragmatic, specialized, and polemical meth-
ods than toward the idealistic, symbolic, and inspirational ones
characteristic of High Romanticism. Although it is easy to think of
exceptions on both sides, generally the High Romantic tends to
beckon man toward a better world by presenting, in Shelley's
phrase, "beautiful idealisms of moral excellence" through a complex of lyricism and iconographic vision; the second-generation
Romantic, or Romantic-Realist, like Charles Dickens, Gustave
Flaubert, or Feodor Dostoevsky labors to carry his readers toward

[16]

a higher view of life by shocking or shaming them into it through a more detailed, more or less dramatic, and very specific portrayal of the present human condition.

To what extent the historical changes to which we have alluded were the cause and to what extent the result of Romanticism's decline from the apogee of the 1820's can never be irrefragably determined. Surely they were in part a cause. Yet High Romanticism was by no means totally lacking in the pragmatic and utilitarian spirit, if this phrase be taken in its most comprehensive meaning. Much confusion undoubtedly arises from too exclusive a focus on the form and method of the great Romantics; in this respect, Shelley is the prime example. With his veils, his caverns, and his spirits, he seems of all his contemporaries to be least in touch with the marketplace and the halls of Parliament; but in truth he probably kept in closer touch with current public affairs than any other writer of equal rank: having once learned how to look, we find Shelley's imagery replete with the specific and the topical as well as with the abstract and the apocalyptic. On the whole, the Romantic poets were more aware, not less, than other men of the particular evils of their day and of the need for definite measures to correct them. In defense of the "so-called Utopians," Jacques Barzun says that "From Byron's speech in the House of Lords on the condition of the hand weavers to Stendhal's dissection of bourgeois greed in *The Red and the Black*, there is hardly a Romanticist—Shelley included—who did not mingle social criticism with his work. If any one school ever invented the social duty of the artist, and kept its critical eye on the contemporary scene, it is the Romantic group of alleged star-gazers." [1]

Apparently many educated readers need to be reminded of this fact; otherwise Barzun, whose career has kept him in close touch with both the academic and the public forum, would not have felt moved to state the case so strongly. On the other hand, those who know intimately the poetry, essays, journals, and letters of the Romantic writers might respond to the passage just quoted with an impatient "Of course, but let's get on with it!" Furthermore, they might argue that it was in the area of practical humanitarianism that High Romanticism was to leave its most profound (though not necessarily most obvious) mark on the following generation of artists. These scholars would be quick to insist that the lines in Hood and Beddoes (and even in Alfred Tennyson and

A. C. Swinburne) which strike us as febrile and shopworn are generally those patently imitative of Romantic imagery and lyricism; but they are without the intellectual and spiritual passion of their models—a passion kindled by genuine concern for man and an acute awareness of the contemporary human condition. Those reasoning on the present lines would maintain, finally, that the most memorable achievements of the "Victorian Romantics" came when they rejected the rented garments of "fashionable" Romanticism and knitted their own by coming to grips with the problems of the human spirit in their own time as the High Romantics had in theirs. It is a long mile indeed between the Byronism of *Poems by Two Brothers* and the truly Tennysonian lineaments of "Ulysses" and "The Palace of Art," to say nothing of "In Memoriam" at its greatest.

I Hood in His Own Time

The career of Thomas Hood could be used to support the preceding argument. His early work—heavily indebted on the humorous and satirical side to Byron and on the serious side to Keats and Shelley—has its moments; but it seldom rises above the level of a fair to good second best. As a humorist and satirist, Hood does far better when he energetically plumbs his own resources (as in "Miss Kilmansegg") to give us his unique blend of the droll, the grotesque, the oblique, the paronomastic. As a serious poet, he is most unforgettable when he strives (as in "The Song of the Shirt" and "The Bridge of Sighs") for an organic rightness of form and feeling rather than when he labors to cast *his* states of mind into Keatsian molds. In short, Hood becomes a good Romantic poet when he insists upon being his own kind of one—for this insistence is the very substratum of Romantic art.

On the sociopolitical side, Hood's career witnessed, though incompletely because of his early death, the progress of the great nineteenth-century reforms for which the Romantics of 1789–1824 had helped brew the ferment. Hood's "The Song of the Shirt" and Dickens' *Oliver Twist* extended in their respective ways the battle lines established by Burns's "Is There for Honest Poverty," Blake's "London," Coleridge's "Ode to the Departing Year," Lord Byron's "Framebreakers'" speech, and the political poems and essays of Shelley. Looking toward our own day, we find that Hood's hectic activities as journalist and editor were geared to, and reflective of, a gradually spreading literacy and, consequently, of the growing role of the man of letters as publicist. Much of the serious work of Hood, especially in his later years, reveals, like that of his friend Dickens, an almost obsessive awareness of the *lacrimae rerum* in *mortalia* and a willingness to use all his energy and talent to set astir in his readers a concern for common mankind that will hopefully issue in beneficent action.

One need be no special pleader for Hood to see this phase of his life as simply heroic. In his last year, desperately ill and hounded almost to distraction by debts and professional obligations, Hood persistently took the field with poems like "The Workhouse Clock," "The Lady's Dream," and "The Lay of the Labourer." That, in turning out such works, Hood was not just being fashionably humanitarian is shown beyond question by the facts attending the genesis of the last-named piece. When Gifford White, a young unemployed farm worker—a "teen-age delinquent," we would probably call him—was sentenced to deportation for life because he had foolishly threatened to burn the property of those who refused him work, Hood not only wrote his "Lay" but accompanied it with an earnest appeal in prose on behalf of White and other victims of the economic juggernaut; and he also made a special plea to the Home Secretary—all at a time when Hood well knew that he needed every ounce of his energy just to remain alive.

II *Hood's Significance Today*

Hood was forced to be, in his own characteristic phrase, "a lively Hood for a livelihood" during most of his career. Until "The Song of the Shirt" appeared, when he had less than a year and a half to live, Hood seems to have been for most of his readers a kind of nineteenth-century James Thurber who gave them witty writings and drawings with just the right balance of whimsy and "bite." But like Thurber—although the comparison can be pushed only so far—Hood was at heart a serious artist and social critic. With a broader perspective than was possible for his contemporaries, we can see him as a comparatively little-known figure in a distinguished company that included Charles Dickens and Thomas Carlyle and that would attract to its standard John Ruskin, Matthew Arnold, William Morris, and George Bernard Shaw. These writers, with many others, proclaimed through their careers an increasing willingness on the part of English artists and intellectuals to carry their talents and their ideals into the theater of public life.

We can be forgiven for speculating that, had Thomas Hood enjoyed better health and lived longer, he would seem more at home in the company mentioned above than he does today. Many readers who have "discovered" Hood would insist that the same might be true with regard to Hood's stature as a pure lyric poet, aside from his humanitarian role. William Michael Rossetti, Mary Russell Mitford, Hugh Walker,[2] and others closer to the age of Hood than we are have considered his poetic talent the finest to emerge between Shelley's time and Tennyson's. In a country so renowned for its singers as England, where even often slighted minor poets can in their best moments often challenge the greatest, this tribute can be no mere damning with faint praise. It might be well worth our trouble to assay it.

CHAPTER 2

The Apprenticeship of a Man of Letters

I *Early Years and First Poems*

WHEN Thomas Hood's father died in 1811, the boy was, like many another middle-class English lad, reluctantly attending a fairly fashionable academy with good prospects of going on to a university and thence to a "gentlemanly" career. The premature death of the elder Hood left the family in difficult financial circumstances, and Thomas was placed in a humbler (although, by his own account, better) school.[1] Unfortunately, he could not remain even here for long; it became absolutely necessary that he prepare for a livelihood in order to support his mother and four sisters. In 1813, then, or possibly a little earlier, young Hood found himself "planted on a counting-house stool, which nevertheless served occasionally for a Pegasus, on three legs, every foot, of course, being a dactyl or a spondee."[2] In the *Comic Annual* for 1833, Hood recorded this struggle between Mammon and the Muse in a Petrarchan sonnet, "Literary Reminiscences":

> Time was, I sat upon a lofty stool,
> At lofty desk, and with a clerkly pen
> Began each morning, at the stroke of ten,
> To write in Bell & Co.'s commercial school;
> In Warnford Court, a shady nook and cool,
> The favourite retreat of merchant men;
> Yet would my quill turn vagrant even then,
> And take stray dips in the Castalian pool.
> Now double entry—now a flowery trope—
> Mingling poetic honey with trade wax—
> Blogg, Brothers—Milton—Grote and Prescott—Pope—
> Bristles—and Hogg—Glyn Mills and Halifax—
> Rogers—and Towgood—Hemp—the Bard of Hope—
> Barilla—Byron—Tallow—Burns—and Flax![3]

Hood's health and, we would surmise, his temperament did not long survive the intellectual smog of the counting house. Showing even in prose a flair for sustained metaphor that betrays the poet, as well as the penchant for whimsical generality characterizing the narrative of his early life, Hood said in the "Literary Reminiscences" that

my appetite failed, and its principal creditor, the stomach, received only an ounce in the pound. My spirits daily became a shade lower—my flesh was held less and less firmly—in short, in the language of the price current, it was expected that I must "submit to a decline." The Doctors who were called in, declared imperatively that a mercantile life would be the death of me—that by so much sitting, I was hatching a whole brood of complaints, and that no Physician would insure me as a merchantman from the Port of London to the next Spring. The Exchange, they said, was against me. . . .[4]

In the late summer or early autumn of 1815, young Thomas Hood made his way, along roads and through crowds still ringing with victory cries over England's triumph at Waterloo, to Dundee, on the eastern coast of Scotland, for the double purpose of visiting relatives and regaining his health.

The rather scanty evidence available—two letters to his aunts and Hood's later reminiscences—suggests that Hood, like Keats, admired Scotland's scenery but was not overfond of her people. At least, however, he was sufficiently interested to begin a satirical "Guide to the City of Dundee," or "Dundee Guide," in eighteenth-century couplets. This first literary effort by Hood of which any trace survives was copied in part in the second of the letters mentioned above, dated December, 1815.[5] The youthful poet hardly equals even the most mediocre efforts of his models (among them, probably, Jonathan Swift, Robert Burns, and Oliver Goldsmith); but, for a boy of sixteen, the "Dundee Guide" seems a notable achievement. Like some of Lord Byron's school verses, it announces a gift for humor and satire of which much might be expected.

Some have thought that Hood contributed some letters signed "Juvenis" to the *Dundee Magazine*, but this name was so frequently used by young writers that the theory rests on shaky internal evidence. A scrapbook of verses and sketches kept by Hood in Scotland has regrettably been lost. We do have, however, the most ambitious literary product of his Scottish sojourn: "The

Bandit," a narrative of 821 lines in Drydenesque couplets (though scarcely with the felicity of Dryden). The theme is that of the "noble outlaw"—one already familiar to the age through such works as Goethe's *Goetz von Berlichingen,* Schiller's *Die Räuber,* Wordsworth's *The Borderers,* and, of course, the enormously popular romances of Scott and Byron. Although a remarkable performance for a scantily educated ex-clerk in his middle teens, "The Bandit" will never claim a place in the preceding list. On the whole, it is decidedly a less promising work than the "Dundee Guide," and indeed it was in the broad genre to which the latter poem belongs that Hood was first to earn fame.

Hood returned to London in the autumn of 1817 with the idea of becoming an engraver, a career doubtless inspired by the success of his uncle, Robert Sands. Hood seems to have pursued this goal with some diligence for several years, but he found enough time to enjoy music, chess, and—of course—writing. Hood even joined a London literary society.[6] A letter written to George Rollo in June, 1821, mentions his hope of bringing out a "little volume" of verse, but we hear no more of it. Hood's mother died about a month later; and, with four sisters to supervise as well as support, Hood had little time for poetry. Nevertheless, this time of personal sorrow for Hood coincided with a major turning point in his career as a man of letters.

II   *The* London Magazine: *1821–1823*

At the time of his mother's death, Hood had already begun an association with the prestigious *London Magazine* as, in his words, "a sort of sub-Editor." [7] In a letter to his friend Rollo, he described his duties in the phrase *"scripsit et sculpsit,"* [8] but Hood must have been more *scriptor* than *sculptor;* at any rate, his contributions to the *London Magazine* came mainly from his pen; indeed, he seems not to have really enjoyed engraving. During its brief life, the *London Magazine* was served by some of the finest talents in English literature: William Hazlitt, Charles Lamb ("Elia"), Thomas De Quincey, and Thomas Carlyle; and even the list of authors of lesser rank who appeared in its pages is quite impressive: Allan Cunningham, John Clare, Henry Francis Cary, John Hamilton Reynolds ("Edward Herbert"), Bryan Waller Procter ("Barry Cornwall"), Horace Smith, Hartley Coleridge, and George Darley. Such familiar masterpieces as Lamb's

"Dream-Children" and "A Dissertation upon Roast Pig" and De Quincey's *Confessions of an English Opium Eater* were first revealed to the world through the pages of the *London Magazine*.

It would be difficult, therefore, to exaggerate the importance of Hood's relationship with the *London Magazine* group in his development as a man of letters. It is very much to Hood's credit that he knew how to value these gifted men and could speak of them without a touch of envy: "But my top-gallant glory was in 'our Contributors!' How I used to look forward to Elia! and backward for Hazlitt, and all round for Edward Herbert, and how I used to *look up* to Allan Cunningham! for at that time the London had a goodly list of writers—a rare company." [9] Hood's verbal etchings of his illustrious colleagues make interesting reading:

> On the right hand then of the Editor sits Elia, of the pleasant smile, and the quick eyes . . . and a wit as quick as his eyes, and sure, as Hazlitt described, to stammer out the best pun and the best remark in the course of the evening. Next to him, shining verdantly out from the grave-coloured suits of the literati, like a patch of turnips amidst stubble and fallow, behold our Jack i' the Green—John Clare! . . .
>
> . . . In opposition to the "extra man's size" of Cunningham, the party in question [Thomas De Quincey] looks almost boyish, partly from being in bulk somewhat beneath Monsieur Quetelet's "Average Man," but still more so from a peculiar delicacy of complexion and smallness of features, which look all the smaller for his wearing, in compliment, probably, to the *Samsons* of Teutonic Literature, his locks unshorn. . . . There is a speculation in the eyes, a curl of the lip, and a general character in the outline, that reminds one of some of the portraits of Voltaire. And a Philosopher he is every inch. . . .[10]

Later Hood returns to Lamb, for whom he, like so many others, felt a special affection. Space allows only a few lines, but the entire section deserves to be read in full:

> How many . . . pleasant reminiscences revive in my memory, whilst thinking of him, like secret writing brought out by the kindly warmth of the fire! . . . If he was intolerant of anything, it was Intolerance. He would have been (if the foundation had existed, save in the fiction of Rabelais,) of the Utopian order of Thelemites. . . . He hated evil speaking, carping, and petty scandal. . . .
>
> . . . Finally he had left behind him his works, a rare legacy! and above all, however much of him had departed, there was still more of him that could not die—for as long as Humanity endures and owns

man's fellowship with man, the spirit of Charles Lamb will still be extant! [11]

The company of men like Lamb and De Quincey must have been as stimulating to Hood professionally as it was personally, for his own labors on the *London Magazine* were prodigious. While not neglecting "The more irksome parts of authorship, such as the correction of the press," which indeed were to Hood "labours of love," [12] his greatest energies went into his own articles and poems. For the time we are concerned only with the latter, and specifically with those contributed during Hood's official connection with the *London*—probably the biennium between June, 1821, and June, 1823.[13] Of these poems, five [14] were to be used later in *Whims and Oddities*, First Series (1826); thirteen in *The Plea of the Midsummer Fairies* (1827); and the remaining nine are listed among Hood's uncollected poems.

The five pieces destined for *Whims and Oddities*, although revealing a certain metrical skill and the penchant for punning and verbal horseplay that was to be so prominent in Hood's work, are not of sufficient merit to detain us. One, "The Stag-Eyed Lady," is interesting as an early example of Hood's talent for pastiche and as a reflector of his readings in contemporary poetry. The work is clearly a spoof of *The Arabian Nights* ("Scheherazade immediately began the following story") and perhaps in a general way of such "Oriental" poems as Thomas Moore's *Lalla Rookh* (both poems have a Hassan), Walter Savage Landor's *Gebir*, and Robert Southey's *Thalaba the Destroyer*. Above all, perhaps, it is a good-natured jab at Lord Byron's so-called Oriental Romances, particularly of *The Giaour*: in Hood's tale, as in Byron's, the Turkish villain is named Hassan; in both, the charming but guilty lady is drowned in a sack. "The Stag-Eyed Lady" is written in Byronic *ottava rima* except for a three-quatrain song at the end, and it contains a number of "Byronic" rhymes ("relate/he sate," "of it/*Profit*," etc.). The poem is clever enough, but Byron need not tremble for his laurels as either humorist or romancer.

There is no Byronic or other buffoonery about the *London Magazine* poems that were used later in *The Plea of the Midsummer Fairies*, Hood's first "serious" book of verse. Four of these are sonnets, one Spenserian ("It is not death") and three Petrarchan

("To Fancy," "To an Enthusiast," and "To Silence"); the last-named poem is by far the best of the lot:

> There is a silence where hath been no sound,
>> There is a silence where no sound may be,
>> In the cold grave—under the deep deep sea,
> Or in wide desert where no life is found,
> Which hath been mute, and still must sleep profound;
>> No voice is hush'd—no life treads silently,
>> But clouds and cloudy shadows wander free,
> That never spoke, over the idle ground:
> But in green ruins, in the desolate walls
>> Of antique palaces, where Man hath been,
> Though the dun fox, or wild hyena, calls,
>> And owls, that flit continually between,
> Shriek to the echo, and the low winds moan,
> There the true Silence is, self-conscious and alone.

The chiastic effect of "where hath been no sound" and "where no sound may be" creates a subtle pianissimo which escapes being a mere display of virtuosity by its *rightness:* the repetition of sounds, especially sibilants, results in a soft, pleasing monotony suggestive of silence itself. In this effect, the poem recalls Keats, as, for example, in the sonnet "To Sleep," which Hood's sonnet resembles also in the almost hermetic quality of the first two lines. The octet reminds us of Keats again with its piling up of words and images that support the theme, as in the opening lines of "Ode on Melancholy," "Ode to a Nightingale," or (again) "To Sleep." The specific Hood conceits themselves are Keatsian: soundlessness, the deep sea, forms of cloud and shadow, profound sleep, the grave.[15]

The sestet of "Silence" is more evocative of Shelley than of Keats. All readers of Shelley's poetry remember his numerous references to clouds, desert wastes, "silence wide and lone," [16] feral beasts and birds—in short, his predilection for what might be called nature *un*methodized, to make free with Pope's phrase. There is a kind of atmospheric similarity between Hood's sonnet and such Shelleyan works as "Ozymandias" and "Alastor" (ll. 78–116). The first three lines of the sestet recall the "green ruin" or "green/And lone ruins" where Laon and Cythna can hear the wailing of the "lean hyenas." [17] Hood's "owls, that flit continually between" the ruins of "antique palaces" are akin to those that "flit/Round the evening tower" in *Epipsychidion*.[18]

These remembrances of Shelley and Keats in Hood's "Silence" are presented not to suggest that Hood wrote the poem with their works open before him but to show that he had much in common with them as a Romantic poet—a point fundamentally more important than the fact that these great writers did exert a powerful influence on Hood. It should be added that several of Keats's sonnets are no better than "Silence" and few of Shelley's as good.

Of the other short poems surveyed here, two—"To an Absentee" and "To a Cold Beauty"—can be dealt with cursorily. Both are, in the telegraphic phrase of old-time magazine film critics, "good of kind." The first resembles many a sentimental lyric on the theme of the beloved person whose worth is recognized too late; the poem is competently written but is not distinguished in any way. "To a Cold Beauty" has more style, but it is that of a bygone day, using as it does the *carpe diem* and *carpe rosam* motifs common to Western poetry since Sappho and favored by Horace, Ausonius, the *Pléiade*, and the Elizabethans, to touch only the peaks. The poem has charm, but it is too derivative to be very memorable. Its stanza, incidentally, is that of Lord Byron's "She Walks in Beauty" except for frequent initial trochees.

Like so many of Hood's serious poems, "Hymn to the Sun" would impress us more if a famous work did not stand in its way. This is not to say that wherever a comparison is forced upon us we necessarily hand the palm to the work bearing the more famous signature; in this case, however, Keats's "Hymn to Apollo," which Hood had not read when he wrote "Hymn to the Sun," [19] clearly outshines the latter. But it is not fair to attempt a genuine value judgment here because the two pieces are so different in tone and—despite the common apostrophic style—even in attitude. Hood's hymn lacks the *excited* utterance of Keats's and is rather nostalgic in its total effect. In this respect, the last two stanzas especially of "Hymn to the Sun" have more in common with Keats's "To Autumn" than with his "Hymn to Apollo."

Hood's poem is a miniature ode, graceful and technically excellent:

> King of the tuneful lyre,
> Still poets' hymns to thee belong;

Though lips are cold
Whereon of old
Thy beams all turn'd to worshipping
　　and song!

Lord of the dreadful bow,
None triumph now for Python's death;
　　But thou dost save
　　From hungry grave
The life that hangs upon a summer
　　breath.

(11. 5–15)

The similarity of metaphors in Hood's "Hymn" and Keats's is too apparent to need comment; we may note also a common striving for an "English Pindaric" effect. Keats's poem is however far more intense than Hood's and more frankly pagan (we can almost see Keats throwing his handful of incense on the altar); Hood is closer to the mannered style of the eighteenth century. The last remark is not meant condescendingly; no nineteenth-century poet would have been ashamed to have written "Hymn to the Sun."

Hood's finest lyric of this period—some would say the best he ever wrote [20]—is "Fair Ines." The first and last stanzas make everyone want to complete the melody:

O saw ye not fair Ines?
She's gone into the West,
To dazzle when the sun is down,
And rob the world of rest:
She took our daylight with her,
The smiles that we love best,
With morning blushes on her cheek,
And pearls upon her breast.

. . . .

Farewell, farewell, fair Ines,
That vessel never bore
So fair a lady on its deck,
Nor danc'd so light before,—
Alas for pleasure on the sea,
And sorrow on the shore!
The smile that blest one lover's heart
Has broken many more!

(11. 1–8, 41–48)

The Apprenticeship of a Man of Letters

The lyric poet who mingles tetrameter and trimeter lines in a regular pattern always risks the danger of becoming singsongy; indeed, even the best poetry so written *can* be read this way. Hood has used, however, some specific devices to prevent such mutilation of his poem. One device is the amphibrach concluding the first line of each stanza, which creates a falling effect and therefore necessitates a slight pause; the line is given a subtle emphasis without a trace of roughness. Furthermore, by placing two trimeter lines at the beginning of each verse, Hood avoids the old tetrameter-trimeter pattern that almost automatically lures most readers into a jingling cadence. More important than these technicalities, however, is the rich but simple and unaffected language of the poem, in which respect it rivals the best lyrics of Burns and Wordsworth. The few "poetic" or older forms are justified by its vaguely Elizabethan flavor—indeed, "Fair Ines" is more Elizabethan than Romantic, to use the latter term in its common "textbook" or chronological sense.

"Fair Ines" recalls the words of Ovid: "So much did art conceal itself." Analysis reveals things not apparent upon a first pleasurable reading of the piece: one is the use of repetition ("And" in the second and fourth stanzas, "But" in the fifth, "Farewell" in the fifth and sixth, and "on the" in the sixth). Simple alliteration is seen in lines three and four of stanza one; three and eight of stanzas three; and five, seven, and eight of stanza five. A subtler alliteration is noted in "Before"—"For fear" (II, 2–3); "And blessed"—"beneath"—"And breathes" (II, 5–7); the words beginning with *w* in III; and "bands"—"And banners" (IV, 3–4). Assonance is also common, as in "not"—"gone" (I, 1–2); "lovely" —"along" (IV, 1–2); "youth"—"plumes"—"beauteous" (IV, 5–7); and "away"—"waiting" (V, 2–3). Both alliteration and assonance were to be prominent features of Hood's lyric verse.

The use of conceits in "Fair Ines" is as memorable as its sound effects (not that the two can be sharply separated, of course). "To dazzle when the sun is down" and "She took our daylight with her" combine concentration and delicacy in admirable balance, and surely few lyricists have packed more ironic pathos into one two-letter word than Hood injects into "If" at the end of stanza four: "It would have been a beauteous dream,/—If it had been no more!" The metaleptic effect of imputing "wrong" to the music that announced Ines' departure (l. 39) is esthetically pleasing and adds to the pathos; equally appealing, if perhaps less subtle, is the double antithesis in the four closing lines of the poem. There is something decidedly Horatian about the tone of "Fair Ines." Its power derives not from the clamant strain of passion so often heard in Romantic and Elizabethan lyric but from a gentle, though deeply felt, melancholy alleviated in some measure by the esthetic pleasure taken in conceits and phrases evoked by the sadness itself.

Value judgments are not easy in so subjective a thing as a Romantic lyric; still, it is pertinent to ask whether we find among the short pieces in this genre addressed to idealized ladies any that are better poetically than "Fair Ines." Among the contestants would be Burns's "Highland Mary" and "Mary Morrison," Wordsworth's "Lucy Poems," Byron's "She Walks in Beauty" and "Maid of Athens," and Shelley's "I Fear Thy Kisses" and "The Indian Serenade." Byron's poems are doubtless more interesting anecdotally and Wordsworth's psychologically; but, if all the works listed were anonymous, how many would be placed above Thomas Hood's "Fair Ines"?

Of the longer *London Magazine* poems that Hood was to include in *The Plea of the Midsummer Fairies*, "The Departure of Summer" is least pleasing to the modern reader. Its 159 couplets leave the impression—one confirmed by extended study of Hood—that his true forte in serious verse is the lyric. This apparent mélange of James Thomson, Leigh Hunt, Milton, and Keats leaves us feeling that its inspiration is too strictly literary and that Hood is forcing himself to write a particular *kind* of poem. Probably it should be considered as an experiment and then forgotten.

"The Two Peacocks of Bedfont," a fanciful tale in twenty-six *ottava rima* stanzas, has more originality than "The Departure of Summer" but cannot be listed with Hood's best serious works. It tells of two vain young village women who are metamorphosed into peacocks after being severely chidden by the pastor of Bedfont. The reader acquainted with Hood's comic gift keeps expecting the sober countenance of this exemplum to crease into a smile, but it never does. Hood, a very moral but not at all pietistic man, seems out of his element in "The Two Peacocks of Bedfont." Nevertheless, the poem has a certain atmospheric authenticity that enables the reader to become part of a simple and vaguely antique world that is for the time quite credible.

Hood's "Ode: Autumn," though frankly an imitation of Keats's "To Autumn," has at least the merit of being, on the whole, a very good one; it would not be too paradoxical to call the work a creative imitation, somewhat like the "translations" of Ezra Pound. A quick collation of the two poems reveals parallels in word and idea that are too obvious to need labored demonstration. It is worthwhile, however, to remark that the final stanza of "Ode: Autumn" is closer in language and thought to Keats's "Ode on Melancholy" than to his piece on autumn and that there are some possible echoes of "La Belle Dame sans Merci":

Hood	*Keats*
"no lonely bird would sing" (1. 3)	"And no birds sing" (1. 4)
"The squirrel gloats on his accomplish'd hoard" (1. 31)	"The squirrel's granary is full" (1. 7)
"a coronal of flowers . . . / Upon her forehead" (11. 50–51)	"I made a garland for her head" (1. 21)
"Whilst all the wither'd world looks drearily" (1. 43)	"The sedge has wither'd from the lake" (11. 3, 58)

The comparison could be extended along more subtle lines by remarking that Keats's Beautiful Lady, like Hood's Autumn, "frame[s] her cloudy prison for the soul" (1. 62). To mention one more Keatsian overtone in "Ode: Autumn," line 32, "The ants have brimm'd their garners with ripe grain," recalls line four of the sonnet "When I Have Fears That I May Cease to Be": "Hold like rich garners the full ripen'd grain."

Compared to Keats's "To Autumn," Hood's "Ode: Autumn" seems a bit overdone. For one thing, the latter is almost twice as long as the former; for another, its language and imagery are generally less simple and concrete. It is unlikely, though, that "Ode: Autumn" would be found disagreeably verbose were there no Keatsian poem to compare it with. In spite of their obvious tangencies, the poems differ in feeling and purpose. Keats's "To Autumn" is a mood piece with no "point" to make; [21] on the other hand, there is a certain tendentiousness in Hood's poem. Like his master, Hood imagizes the mellow fruitfulness, the plethoric fullness, and the dreamy lassitude of autumn. But the mood of privation and melancholy, subtly hinted at by Keats in the final stanza of "To Autumn," is the dominant key in Hood's treatment.

The note of darkness is sounded faintly even in the first stanza of "Ode: Autumn": "no lonely bird would sing / Into his hollow ear from woods forlorn" (11. 3–4). As the piece progresses, we see that Hood stresses the *ubi sunt* theme more than Keats and that his use of it is more traditional. "Where are the songs of Summer?" (1. 9) is in a very different vein from Keats's "Where are the songs of Spring?" (1. 23). For Keats, the Lydian melodies of fall are "abundant recompense" for the Phrygian tunes of spring; for Hood, the beauty and joy have fled with the "merry birds" of summer, leaving the world to the savage, predatory owls (11. 13–17). In the stanza following, the *ubi sunt* formula is used twice more to convey conventional feelings of sadness and loss; and Hood intensifies this feeling in stanza four by blending the mood and the season into one figure: "But here the Autumn melancholy dwells, / And sighs her tearful spells" (11. 36–37). As we penetrate the final stanza, so suggestive of Keats's "Ode on Melancholy," we feel that Hood's poem is a fusion of two subjects treated—superbly, of course—in separate poems by Keats.

The blending of melancholy with the sights and sounds of autumn gives organic shape to "Ode: Autumn." The connection is made in the first stanza by the use of "lonely" and "forlorn"; in the second, the sense of mournfulness at summer's departure is imagized through the song birds and owls; in the third, the idea is sustained and strengthened by the repetition of "Where are . . . ?," the comparison of autumn's conquest to the rape of Proserpine, and the suggestion of death in the skeletal trees. Hood next shows the flexibility of his poetic strategy by deliberately introducing images normally used to embody the fullness and ripeness of autumn, but only to strip his subject of the charming features falsely (as he thinks) associated with it. The squirrel, the bee, and the ant have their winter hoards, but these are summer's fruits, and these lively creatures are not now part of the scene; like the blooms and greenery, they belong with the life that has fled and not with the death or near-death that remains. In Keats's "To Autumn," the swallows are gathered in the sky prior to their departure, but this fact is not explicitly mentioned and the birds still add charm to the scene; in Hood's poem they have "wing'd across the main," and "Autumn melancholy," left

"Alone, alone," tearfully "reckons up the dead and gone" (ll. 35–41). The gradation of imagery leading to this syncrasy of natural phenomenon and human feeling has been made with skill and propriety.

In the final stanza, Hood intensifies this relationship, broadens the philosophical scope of the poem by envisioning the death of the summer rose as the death of Beauty herself, and concludes the piece with a tasteful union of deep emotion and somber restraint through the use of a ceremonial anaphora:

> Enough of bitter fruits the earth doth bear,—
> Enough of chilly droppings for her bowl;
> Enough of fear and shadowy despair,
> To frame her cloudy prison for the soul!
>
> (ll. 59–62)

Hood has fully, and for the most part expertly, accomplished his purpose, and "Ode: Autumn" must be reckoned a successful poem.

None of the remaining nine poems [22] published by Hood in the *London Magazine* during his employment with it is important enough to be analyzed in this survey of his early work. But two poems published in the *New Monthly Magazine* after Hood's departure from the *London*, both rather experimental in character, are worth a brief look. The first, "The Two Swans: A Fairy Tale," written in competent Spenserian stanzas, is fairly impressive as a tour de force because some authentic echoes of Spenser are sounded with a minimal use of archaic language. The second, "Ode on a Distant Prospect of Clapham Academy," is a mischievous yet somehow touching parody of Thomas Gray's famous "Ode on a Distant Prospect of Eton College" that announces Hood's facility in this genre of light poetry.

The purpose of this chapter has been chiefly to trace Hood's early development as a poet, and it is evident that his position on the staff of the *London Magazine* gave him many opportunities to practice his craft. It must not be thought, however, that he was employed by the *London* as a kind of poet-in-residence. Besides having many routine editorial duties, Hood also contributed essays, reviews, and the like. Some of these, being unsigned or ambiguously signed, are difficult to identify with certainty, and most are unimportant in themselves. One, "A Sentimental Journey from Islington to Waterloo Bridge" (examined in Chapter 5), foreshadows the Sternesque flavor of much of Hood's later prose. Certainly, his most sheerly entertaining offerings to the *London Magazine* were under the caption of "The Lion's Head," a column in which Hood wrote witty and incisive replies to the journal's correspondents (some of them possibly imaginary). A few examples follow: [23]

Lines by "A Student in the Inner Temple" are received. *Curia advisare vult*.[24]

We are compelled to announce to E. R. that "The Storm" is blown over.

Colin has sent us a Summer Pastoral, and says he can supply us with one every month. Has he always got sheep in his *pen?*

Beta's . . . poem on *Fame* will bring neither him nor us any.

W.'s "Night" is too long, for the moon rises twice in it.

We look for very light articles from anonymous contributors who forget to pay the postage.

To Y. and Y. No—A word to the Y.'s!

T. says his tail is out of his own head: is he a tadpole?

The verve and relish of these sallies reveal unmistakably a man who loves his work; the type of humor displayed, especially the fondness for puns, indicates the general route of Hood's first fame as a writer.

The two years that Thomas Hood spent with the *London Magazine*, although they seem to have terminated rather unhappily,[25] had been priceless ones for him; they amounted, in effect, to a salaried apprenticeship of a man of letters. Not often is a young writer placed in a situation where he is not only encouraged but paid (however moderately) to mature his talent. It is possible that when Hood left the *London*—surely it was not much later— he was already planning his first book of verse.

CHAPTER 3

"A Lively Hood for a Livelihood"

I Odes and Addresses to Great People

THOMAS HOOD'S first book of poems, *Odes and Addresses to Great People* (1825), established him solidly as a comic poet and public entertainer. Since virtually all the techniques that dominate the bulk of Hood's poetry are introduced in this volume, we must give closer attention to its contents than their poetic merit sometimes entitles them to.

A kind of comic forerunner of Browning's *Parleyings, Odes and Addresses* was conceived by Hood in 1824, perhaps while he was convalescing from illness at Hastings. Hood wrote to his friend John Hamilton Reynolds [1] in the summer of that year to invite him to join the venture, and Reynolds responded eagerly. Actual collaboration seems to have begun in August, and the resulting fifteen poems—nine by Hood, five by Reynolds, and one written jointly [2]—appeared anonymously in February, 1825. The book was an instant success—a triumph doubly delightful to Hood since his bright prospects as an author made possible his marriage to Jane Reynolds, his collaborator's sister. Despite the misgivings of some of Hood's friends that he was in danger of squandering his talent on trivia,[3] the reception given *Odes and Addresses* was doubtless sheer intoxication to a young man anxious to make his way in the literary world.

We are concerned only with the poems that are wholly Hood's and with the one (the last one in the following list) done in collaboration with his partner: "Ode to Mr. Graham, the Aeronaut," "A *Friendly* Address to Mrs. Fry *in* Newgate," "Ode to Richard Martin, Esquire, M.P. for Galway," "Ode to the Great Unknown," "Ode to Joseph Grimaldi, senior," "An Address to the Steam Washing Company," "Ode to Captain Parry," "Ode to W. Kitchener, M.D.," [4] "Ode to H. Bodkin, Esq.," and "Address to Maria

Darlington, on her return to the Stage." [5] The "Great People" who
are the subjects of these poems are a motley crew. Of the nine,
only Sir Walter Scott, the "Great Unknown," would be *known* to
most readers today; but some would recognize Grimaldi, the famous clown, and Mrs. Fry, the prison reformer. As for the rest, it
is enough to know the following facts: Mr. Graham won fame by
a sensational balloon ascent in 1823; Richard Martin was the first
member of Parliament to agitate successfully for laws protecting
animals; Captain (Sir William E.) Parry was an arctic explorer;
Dr. William Kitchiner, who yearned to be a Leonardo *redivivus,*
had written among other things *The Cook's Oracle* (hence Hood's
changing the name to Kitchener); Hood's subtitle identifies H.
Bodkin as "Secretary to the Society for the Suppression of Mendicity"; Maria Darlington was a well-known actress.

In the beautifully apposite phrase of Hood's friend Lamb, the
poems in *Odes and Addresses* are "hearty, good-natured things."
Although often called "satires," the term is of doubtful accuracy:
the book has its satirical moments; but, as a whole, it is satirical
only in the sense that any work making light of serious things is
so. With possible, though slight, exceptions in the "Bodkin" and
"Steam Washing Company" pieces, *Odes and Addresses* aims only
at entertaining the reader. Some genuine criticism of Scott's
novels is at least implied in "Ode to the Great Unknown," but
criticism is not necessarily satire simply because it wears the
mask of harlequin. The influence of Byron, and to a slighter extent of Swift and others, is seen throughout the book; the tone,
however, is much closer to that of Sterne and Lamb, both favorites of Hood, or of Burns at his most genial. It is revealing that
Coleridge immediately identified *Lamb* as the author of *Odes
and Addresses.*[6] Lamb, correcting Coleridge, wrote "They are
hearty, good-natured things, and I would put my name to 'em
cheerfully. . . . Hood will be gratified, as much as I am, by your
mistake." [7] Naturally Hood *was* gratified, but not because he had
consciously imitated Lamb. Quite likely the playful hand of
Lamb indirectly influenced the *Odes and Addresses,* but it is impossible to say how much Hood owed to him and how much to
Sterne, Swift, Byron, Moore, Hunt, Goldsmith, and others. The
Lambian qualities of the work are probably due as much to temperamental consanguinity as to direct influence. Both Lamb and

Hood were far more given to whimsicality, often poignantly edged with melancholy, than to savage mockery.

In form, the poems in *Odes and Addresses* show considerable variety. Seven of these are dignified as "Odes"; and, following Hood's own mock-Classical bent, we can combine whimsy and accuracy in classifying them as monostrophic or polystrophic. The first of these labels is appropriate for the odes to Graham, Grimaldi, Parry, and Bodkin. All except the last use a six-line stanza predominantly in iambic tetrameter. In the odes to Graham and Parry, the third and sixth lines have three feet and the others four, rhyming *aabccb;* the "Ode to H. Bodkin" is in quatrains of alternating tetrameters and trimeters with the pattern *abcb;* the Grimaldi ode is in consistent tetrameters that rhyme *ababcc*. The last-named work recalls the measure of Byron's "The Isles of Greece," and the others echo the sestets and quatrains of Coleridge's "The Rime of the Ancient Mariner"; but there is no way of knowing whether or not Hood was aiming at these similarities or was even aware of them.

The polystrophic odes—those to Martin, the "Great Unknown," and Kitchiner—show more originality of form than the others. They vary greatly in length, having, respectively, 79, 272, and 186 lines, as well as in stanza-length within each poem. In "Ode to the Great Unknown" there is a differential of eighteen lines between the shortest and the longest stanzas. Hood mixes lines of from two to five feet (usually iambic), with skillful pacing, to achieve a kind of mock-Pindaric effect (as the term "Pindaric" is commonly construed by non-Classical readers); and both form and tone are characteristic of the polystrophic odes.

> How many sing of wars,
> Of Greek and Trojan jars—
> The butcheries of men!
> The Muse hath a 'Perpetual Ruby Pen!'
> Dabbling with heroes and the blood they spill;
> But no one sings the man
> That, like a pelican,
> Nourishes Pity with his tender *Bill!*
>
> Thou Wilberforce of hacks!
> Of whites as well as blacks,
> Pyebald and dapple gray,
> Chestnut and bay—

> No poet's eulogy thy name adorns!
>> But oxen, from the fens,
>> Sheep—in their pens,
> Praise thee, and red cows with their winding horns!
>> Thou art sung on brutal pipes!
>>> ("Ode to Richard Martin," ll. 1–17)

The three "Addresses" show some interesting uses of and improvisations upon already familiar patterns, much as in the monostrophic odes. "An Address to the Steam Washing Company" is mainly in anapestic tetrameter couplets, which Hood quite likely learned from Scott and Byron. In these poets, however, the measure usually sounds a martial strain, specifically the hoofbeats of charging horses, as in Scott's "Lochinvar" and "Bonny Dundee" or Byron's "The Destruction of Sennacherib." Since the tone of Hood's novelty piece is ostensibly rather militant, and since the anapest might simulate the "one, two, THREE" of either the washboard or the steam piston, it seems likely that metrical parody is intended:

> From your new Surrey Geisers all foaming and hot,—
> That soft 'simmer's sang' so endear'd to the Scot—
> If your hands may stand still, or your steam without danger,
> If your suds will not cool, and a mere simple stranger,
> Both to you and to washing, may put in a rub,—
> O wipe out your Amazon arms from the tub,—
>> (ll. 9–14)

The poem proper is followed by a "documentary" piece, "Letter of Remonstrance from Bridget Jones to the Noblemen and Gentlemen Forming the Washing Committee," which has 105 lines of doggerel couplets so studiedly atrocious that they command respect as a dialectal, quasi-poetic tour de force, although we would prefer less abundant evidence of Hood's virtuosity. The lines defy metrical analysis, or at least classification: "I'm Certain sure Enuff your Ann Sisters had no stream Ingins, that's Flat,— / But I Warrant your Four Fathers went as Tidy and gentlemanny for all that" (ll. 7–8). It is easy to see that Hood would have a good deal to live down when he came to don the robe of a serious poet.

The "Address to Mrs. Fry" uses the *ottava rima* form, surely reflecting Hood's admiration for the mature satires of Byron. (He might also have seen the *ottava rima* poems of William Tennant, John Hookham Frere, and William Stewart Rose.) The "Address to Maria Darlington" is something of a formal improvisation: it has nine eight-line stanzas all rhyming *ababcdcd* except the second (which has *ababcccc*), with anapestic trimeter dominating the metrical structure. Although it sounds somewhat like Byronic *ottava rima* gone wrong, the over-all effect is pleasing.

In style and treatment, the *Odes and Addresses* show no radical departures from historic English satire and comic verse. The mock-Classical is fairly common; the first two stanzas of "Ode to Richard Martin," for example, manage to burlesque simultaneously epic, tragedy, and pastoral. In "An Address to the Steam Washing Company," the homeliness of the subject makes the mock-Classic touch practically irresistible. Hood achieves a facetiously elevated style by using exhortatory "O's" and "Ah's," a Popean "Lo, . . . the poor laundress," the venerable *ubi sunt* motif, and references to the Amazons, Aurora, and Venus (11. 7, 15, 92, 53, 61 ff., 14, 29, 31). Another notable bit of clowning with Classic matter and style occurs in the "Ode to W. Kitchener." Longing (he says) for a view of the great man's head on a (book) plate, the poet is inspired to visualize this object as

> . . . Orpheus-like,—fresh from thy dying strains,
>   Of music,—Epping luxuries of sound,
>   As Milton says, 'in many a bout
>   O linked sweetness long drawn out,'
> Whilst all thy tame stuffed leopards listen'd round! [8]
>   (11. 37–41)

The allusion to the head of Orpheus, severed by the Thracian maidens but still singing as it floats down the Hebrus, is obviously a bit labored but just as obviously ingenious. More amusing is simply the *idea* of comparing the strains of Orpheus (wild, primitive, unearthly) with "Epping luxuries of sound" (tame, ultragenteel, mundane). Hood's merciless portrayal of the doctor's admirers as "tame, stuffed leopards" at once brings to mind the feral, lissome attendants of Orpheus and Dionysus; the devastating contrast could hardly be surpassed by Lord Byron himself.

Speaking of Byron, we see his probable influence everywhere in the *Odes and Addresses*. Byronic rhymes [9] are particularly in evidence: "rainbow"—"vain, go" ("Mrs. Fry," ll. 18, 20); "preys in"—"raisin" (*ibid.*, ll. 74, 76); "bolt on"—"Colton" ("The Great Unknown," ll. 82, 84); "fit on"—"Britton" (*ibid.*, ll. 124–25); "pious Row"—"his Co." ("Captain Parry," ll. 17, 20); "ven'son"—"pens on" (*ibid.*, ll. 18–19); "sublime it"—"climate" (*ibid.*, ll. 169–70); "opodeldock"—"smell dock" (*ibid.*, ll. 184–85). The list could be expanded, but a few facetious rhymes go a long way when listed out of context. Encountered more normally, they add much to the fun of reading *Odes and Addresses*.

Sometimes Hood is quite Byronesque in treating a supposedly grand subject with skepticism. When Hood asks "Oh! what is glory?—what is fame? / Hark to the little mob's acclaim" ("Mr. Graham," ll. 73–74), it is impossible not to think of Byron's many lines on the same subject, as in "And glory long has made the sages smile; / 'Tis something, nothing, words, illusion, wind" (*Don Juan*, III, xc). Similarly, both authors are fond of joshing prominent people; in this respect, the most patently Byronic poem in the *Odes and Addresses* is the "*Friendly* Address to Mrs. Fry *in* Newgate." A collation by the reader of the seventh, eleventh, and seventeenth stanzas of this *ottava rima* poem with *Don Juan*, X, lxxxv–lxxxvii, will make further comment unnecessary.

Hood, like Byron, can be humorously chatty about his problems as a poet and his troubles with other writers, as in the "Ode to Mr. Graham":

> Campbell—(you cannot see him here)—
> Hath scorn'd my *lays*:—do his appear
>   Such great eggs from the sky?—
> And Longman, and his lengthy Co.
> Long, only, in a little Row,
>   Have thrust my poems by!
>   (ll. 151–56) [10]

There is no striking parallel with Byron here, but there is a broad kinship with such passages as *Don Juan*, IV, iii–vii. The kinship is more apparent when Hood levels a full volley at his contemporaries:

> A fig for Southey's Laureat lore!—
> What's Rogers here?—Who cares for Moore
> That hears the Angels sing!—
> . . . .

"A Lively Hood for a Livelihood"

> Come:—what d'ye think of Jeffrey, sir?
> Is Gifford such a Gulliver
>   In Lilliput's Review,
> That like Colossus he should stride
> Certain small brazen inches wide
>   For poets to pass through?
>   ("Mr. Graham," ll. 88–90, 109–14)

The tone of these verses approaches that of Byron's *English Bards and Scotch Reviewers;* the two authors even single out some of the same victims (one not noted above is George Croly, in line 121). Both are hard on Southey, whom Hood slaps again in the "Ode to Mr. Martin." Hood may be milder than Byron, but he is clearly in the same camp with the author of *English Bards,* "The Vision of Judgment," and *Don Juan.*[11] We may compare, for example, Hood's reference to Southey's "Pegasus" as an "ancient hackney" with Byron's to the "spavin'd dactyls" of the Laureate's verse and to the "jaded Pegasus" of mediocre scribblers, including Southey.[12] Both poets are scornful of Southey's laureateship and of the post itself: Hood's words on the subject quoted earlier in this paragraph agree perfectly with Byron's "Bob Southey! You're a poet—Poet-laureate, / And representative of all the race" (*Don Juan,* Dedication, ll. 1–2).

Recalling the young Byron's unkind words about Sir Walter Scott in *English Bards and Scotch Reviewers,* we might expect to see some Byronic qualities in "Ode to the Great Unknown." Actually, there is little to compare, aside from a common subject and a few similar allusions to knights, sprites, and wizards. Indeed, precisely because they *are* on a common subject, a comparison of the poems tells us more of the differences between Byron and Hood than of their resemblances. For one thing, of course, Hood was not angry when he wrote his poem, as Byron was. But, aside from this circumstantial fact, Hood was simply more good-natured than Byron; he was also more truly sophisticated and urbane. The fact that Hood was nearly twenty-six and Byron only twenty-one when they wrote their respective pieces does not explain away this point—as an examination of the poems written by Lord Byron at twenty-six easily show. We must not think of the Hood of *Odes and Addresses* as an imitator of *English Bards* and *Don Juan;* for, even when he uses facetious rhymes or jabs at Southey, Hood reminds us much less of the Juvenalian

master of devastating exposé than of the Montaignesque figure
that Byron becomes in his more genial moments. Indeed, Hood's
attitude and tone are usually less suggestive of Byron's great
satires than of less famous and more "relaxed" works like "Paren-
thetical Address," "Ballad to the Tune of 'Sally in Our Alley,'"
"Another Simple Ballat," "New Song to the Tune of 'Whare Hae
Ye Ben a'Day,'" "My Dear Mr. Murray," and "Dear Doctor, I
Have Read Your Play"—poems perhaps never read by Hood.

To summarize and generalize, there can be no doubt that Lord
Byron left his mark on Hood's *Odes and Addresses,* but it does
not follow that every comical or satirical element in the book
reflects Byronic influence. It might be instructive to explore the
possibility of Hood's indebtedness to Frere, Moore, Peacock, and
other contemporaries, not to mention older figures. Moreover,
similarity does not always show indebtedness; as Montaigne said,
"It is no more according to Plato than it is according to me." One
thing at least is sure: the most distinctive feature of the *Odes and
Addresses* (as of all his humorous poetry)—the use of the pun—
is decidedly Hood's.[13]

A listing of word plays might not strike the reader as a special
treat. Since, however, Hood's supremacy as a punster is a point on
which nearly all of his critics agree, it is important to take a quick
look at his early published efforts. Fortunately, Hood's puns are,
though admittedly too numerous, generally successful enough to
sustain the reader's tolerance. The following selections from *Odes
and Addresses* make up a representative group.

Frequently Hood uses the simple equivoque, in which some
common word is used twice with very different meanings:

> Witness their goodly labours one by one!
> *Russet* makes garments for the needy poor—
> *Dove-colour* preaches love to all—and *dun*
> Calls every day at Charity's street-door—
> *Brown* studies scripture, and bids woman shun
> All gaudy furnishing—*olive* doth pour
> Oil into wounds: and *drab* and *slate* supply
> Scholar and book in Newgate, Mrs. Fry!
> ("Mrs. Fry," ll. 41–48)

Among other examples of the equivoque are:

> Or found new ways for ships to shape,
> Instead of winding round the Cape,
> A short cut thro' the collar!
>> ("Captain Parry," 11. 16–18)

> Oh, rather thy whole proper length reveal,
> Standing like Fortune,—on the jack—thy wheel.
> (Thou art, like Fortune, full of chops and changes,
> Thou hast a fillet too before thine eye!)
> Scanning our kitchen, and our vocal ranges,
> As tho' it were the same to sing or fry—
> Nay, so it is—hear how Miss Paton's throat
> Makes 'fritters' of a note!
>> ("W. Kitchener," 11. 42–49)

(Dr. "Kitchener" fancied himself not only a culinary expert but a musician.)

Similar to the puns just noted are those featuring words slightly unlike in form but homonymous in sound, as in the play on "poles" and *"poll"* in lines 128 and 132 of "Captain Parry" or in "but it will cost its price, / To give a good, round, real *cheque* to Vice!" ("Mrs. Fry," 11. 143–44). Occasionally such puns are "literary," but they are seldom so learned as to puzzle a moderately well-read person:

> The cruel Jarvy hast thou summon'd oft,
> Enforcing mercy on the coarse Yahoo,
> That thought his horse the *courser* of the two—
> Whilst Swift smiled down aloft!—
>> ("Richard Martin," 11. 29–32)

> And Man and Horse go half and half,
> As if their griefs met in a common *Centaur!*
>> ("Richard Martin," 11. 78–79)

> I like thy Landlord's Tales!—I like that Idol
> Of love and Lammermoor—the blue-eyed maid
> That led to church the mounted cavalcade,
> And then pull'd up with such a bloody bridal!
> Throwing equestrian Hymen on his haunches—
>> ("The Great Unknown," 11. 151–55)

The specimens of Hood's punnic art thus far noted have a certain timelessness: most can be understood as easily now as in 1825.

On the other hand, many of those depending on proper names as such would remain sepulchered for many years were it not for editorial notes; for even a word play like the following is of uneasy immortality:

> What is that seeming tea-urn there?
> That fairy dome, St. Paul's!—I swear,
> Wren must have been a Wren!—
> ("Mr. Graham," 11. 31–33)

The great architect Sir Christopher Wren is not forgotten, but his name is no longer a household word. Even more doubtful puns of the same kind are these from "Joseph Grimaldi": "One only— (Champion of the ring) / Could ever make his Winter,—Spring!"; "'sic transit gloria *Munden!*'"; "There's *Quick,* might just as well be dead!" (11. 71–72,[14] 82, 96). Thomas Winter, a famed prize-fighter, boxed under the name of Tom Spring; Joe Munden was, like Grimaldi, a leading clown; Quick was a well-known actor of the day. The real gem of the lot, earning from Coleridge the accolade of "transcendent," [15] is in "Mrs. Fry": "But I don't like your Newgatory teaching" (1. 104). At this point in the poem, every reader will fortunately understand the pun—provided, of course, that he knows the word "nugatory."

In justice to Hood, something should be said of the nonpunnic humor in the ten poems covered by this survey, and his literary allusions generally provide the best examples. Before proceeding to these, however, let us note that, for a nonuniversity man with comparatively little formal schooling, Hood shows a wide range of reading. That he kept abreast of his contemporaries is shown by his direct or indirect references to William Wordsworth, Mary Shelley, Thomas Medwin, William Lisle Bowles, William Cobbett, and John Clare, besides those mentioned earlier in this section. Among older writers (that is, those who died before 1800) quoted, paraphrased, or alluded to in *Odes and Addresses* are Robert Burns, Thomas Chatterton, Edward Young, Georges Buffon, David Hume, Joseph Addison, Isaac Watts, Jonathan Swift, Alexander Pope, George Farquhar, John Dryden, John Milton, William Shakespeare, and Michel de Montaigne. Nor are the Classics slighted: although only five great Classical authors are named (Homer, Plato, Catullus, Cato, and Saint Augustine), altogether there are at least twenty-five echoes of Classical literature, my-

thology, or history, to say nothing of occasional flickers of a mock-
Classical tone.

That perennial favorite of literary wagsters, Shakespeare, is
summoned by Hood far oftener than any other single writer. The
Shakespearean echoes in "Joseph Grimaldi" illustrate Hood's deft
use of literary allusion for humorous effect:

> All youth—all ages—yet to be,
> Shall have a heavy miss of thee!
>
> Thou didst not preach to make us wise—
>   Thou hadst no finger in our schooling—
> Thou didst not 'lure us to the skies'—[16]
> Thy simple, simple trade was—Fooling!
> And yet, Heav'n knows! we could—we can
> Much 'better spare a better man!' [17]
>
>   (11.11–18)

Hood's *bon mot* proves that Grimaldi, like Falstaff, is "not only
witty . . . but the cause that wit is in other men" (*Henry IV, Part
I*, I.ii. 11–12). The comparison of Grimaldi with Yorick later in the
poem (11. 45–46) is splendidly apt, for Hood's whole tribute to
the great clown could not be better epitomized than by the words
"A fellow of infinite jest, of most excellent fancy" (*Hamlet*, V.i.
203–4)—provided, of course, that enacted jests and fancies be
given equal place with verbal ones.

The parodic Shakespearean tones in "H. Bodkin" also deserve
mention: "Hail, King of Shreds and Patches, Hail," "Thou Dog in
office," and "What ills can mortals have, they can't / With a bare
Bodkin end?" (11. 1, 2, 51–52). Almost alone among the *Odes and
Addresses*—"almost" because some might see in "The Steam Washing Company" a crude ancestor of "The Song of the Shirt"—the
"Ode to H. Bodkin, Esq." rings with a tone that foreshadows
Hood's later protest poems. The studiedly bathetic comparison of
Bodkin to Claudius (and perhaps to Macbeth) is comical enough,
but "Dog in office" is raw satirical invective, especially if we think
of the painful scene in *King Lear* which probably suggested it to
Hood.[18] The play on Bodkin's name in line 52 almost merits the
revival of Coleridge's word "transcendent"—not just because of its
cleverness or its facility, with the bonus of imaginative grotes-
querie—but because of its extraordinary aptness. The pun ex-

presses with unique force Hood's feelings about the attitude toward the poor reflected by Bodkin and his "Society for the Suppression of Mendicity"—that, in the words of Dickens's Scrooge, "If they had rather die . . . they had better do it, and decrease the surplus population."

As a book of poetry in its own right, not as a forerunner of Hood's future poetry, Odes and Addresses, like all humorous works on topical subjects, is difficult to assay objectively. Most of the poems in this volume are about persons or subjects that today's reader knows—or cares—little about. We have seen that many of the jokes and puns are still funny, but many depend on specialized information. For example, in reading the "Ode to W. Kitchener" we appreciate several of Hood's witticisms, but on the whole we are apt to find his cleverness about an obscure eccentric and his cookbook somewhat wearisome. There can be good and bad poems on the order of "W. Kitchener"; this one, by virtue of its wit and technical proficiency, deserves the label of good. The fact remains, however, that it is largely a museum piece. Topical humor, unsupported by something larger than itself, is seldom long-lived unless vitalized by lucky accident. Indeed, most humorous literature, even the best, must to a degree sacrifice permanent appeal to immediate effect. This is truer of Hood's lighter works than of those by more celebrated artists partly because his native gifts were smaller than theirs. Those readers who know Hood at his best, however, maintain that at least part of the reason for the frothy, "gossip column" quality pervading the Odes and Addresses is found in the circumstances that forced the author to be "A Lively Hood for a Livelihood."

II Whims and Oddities, First Series

Not slow to capitalize on the success scored by Odes and Addresses to Great People, Hood began assembling a second crowd-pleaser. This, the Whims and Oddities, First Series, containing both verse and prose pieces, appeared late in 1826. The book is well named, although Whims and Trivialities would serve as well, a judgment evidenced by the comparatively light treatment of its contents in this chapter: only eleven of its twenty-one poems are considered, and some of these very briefly.[19]

Two of these poems, "A Valentine" and "Love," are in ottava rima and are—predictably—very much in Lord Byron's vein. The first brings to mind Julia's farewell to Juan in Canto I of *Don Juan,* but in this case Hood's touch is more facetiously Byronic than the master's own. There is also a suggestion of Byron's "Fare Thee Well" and a slighter, though clearly discernible, one of the dark hero of *Manfred* and similar works. Of "Love," it is enough to say that the poem appears to be a rather slight shadow cast by Byron's words on the subject in the third and fourth cantos of *Don Juan.*

"The Fall of the Deer," thirty-six pseudo-Elizabethan lines of tour de force, deserves mention as evidence of Hood's versatility—something of which we are constantly reminded. The poem's general content, and especially the play on "sore" in lines 27–28 ("and they / Pushing him sore, he pusheth sore"), suggest that the work was inspired by Holofernes' "extemporal epitaph on the death of the deer" in Shakespeare's *Love's Labour's Lost* (IV. ii. 51–52, 58–63). Another work that can be largely written off as an interesting experiment is "She Is Far from the Land," a Gilbert-and-Sullivanesque piece that uses dactyllic dimeter throughout to convey excitement and urgency.

"A Winter Nosegay" and "Remonstratory Ode from the Elephant at Exeter Change" press back into service the irregular but generally well-controlled odic form already familiar to us through the *Odes and Addresses.* The blending of plaintiveness and humor in "A Winter Nosegay" gives it a certain modest charm. The "Remonstratory Ode" is, like its subject, somewhat ponderous—too much so (148 lines) to show at best advantage the whimsical inventiveness and good humor that we expect from Hood.

Two works in ballad quatrains that must be rated high within their lackluster genre—the pun-laden burlesque of a melancholy folk ballad—are "Faithless Sally Brown" and "Faithless Nelly Gray." [20] Both of these "exquisite *morceaux*" [21] are quite funny; both, at the same time, reveal a penchant for "gallows-humor" that becomes more and more prominent in Hood's poetry:

> Ben Battle was a soldier bold,
>   And used to war's alarms:
> But a cannon-ball took off his legs,
>   So he laid down his arms!
> ("Faithless Nelly Gray," ll. 1–4)

Another poem roughly in the same class as these is "The Mermaid of Margate," a tale in thirty-one quatrains about a fishmonger's near-fatal love affair with a mermaid. Many singers have invoked Momus in treating the mortal-immortal theme; Hood's poem is akin to the folksong "The Eddystone Light" and to Charles Godfrey Leland's "Ballad of the Mermaid" (a parody of Heinrich Heine's "The Lorelei").

Literary parody is represented by two pieces in *Whims and Oddities*, "The Irish Schoolmaster" and "The Sea-Spell." The first is clearly intended, in part at least, as a parody of William Shenstone's "The Schoolmistress." Both poets describe in Spenserian stanzas a down-at-heel country school supervised by a severe but pathetic pedagogue whose academic halls are frequented by chickens (and, in Hood's version, even by a pig), who are only slightly less avid for learning than the pupils. "The Irish Schoolmaster" is to some extent a satirical reminiscence of the author's own school days, although the harsh and unkempt Dominie of the poem resembles only vaguely the "decayed" but "worthy" one of the school that Hood last attended; the unkindlier parts of the poem are probably directed at the schools in which he had earlier suffered.[22] The poem is a clever and amusing piece of its kind.

"The Sea-Spell," consisting of twenty-one six-line stanzas like those in Coleridge's "The Rime of the Ancient Mariner," is a moderately funny burlesquing of that work; but it is not one of Hood's best parodic efforts. In it, a seaman counts upon his lucky caul to preserve him from drowning; the ocean, unfortunately, does not "heed his *caul*" (1. 126). There are several parallels with Coleridge in "The Sea-Spell," but they hardly do justice to Hood's talent. From the modern reader's viewpoint, the poem is only a fair success; for Hood's contemporaries, however, "The Sea-Spell" was a delightful treat, and the volume in which it appeared was the author's second triumph within two years.

Indeed, it appeared that Hood had taken an unquestioned place as one of the most successful writers of his day. Even the formidable *Blackwood's Magazine*, admittedly looking for a "new Cockney" to use its "knout" upon, praised the work generously, comparing Hood to Addison, Goldsmith, and Lamb and finding Hood's "The Last Man" far better than comparable works by Lord Byron, Campbell, and Mrs. Shelley.[23] Such acclaim encouraged Hood to issue a *Second Series* of the work in 1827; and, meanwhile, it was widely imitated—the surest sign of commercial success. Additional proof that Hood had "arrived" in the literary world was his appointment as dramatic critic for the new periodical *Atlas*.[24]

In the literary as in the theatrical world, the successful comic performer suffers from a feeling of insufficiency and yearns to fulfill himself as a serious artist. This statement is the more apt to be true when, as in Hood's case, the person concerned is not truly a jester at the deepest level of his being. Those who know Hood best find something decidedly painful in the forced lightness with which he undercuts his own aspirations and abilities in the Preface to his first volume of *Whims and Oddities*: "At a future time, the Press may be troubled with some things of a more serious tone and purpose,—which the Author has resolved upon publishing, in despite of the advice of certain critical friends. His forte, they say, is decidedly humourous: but a gentleman cannot always be breathing his comic vein." [25] Hood's essential earnestness in this statement was proved by his publication of the two volumes of *National Tales* in February, 1827. Although more must be said of the *Tales* in Chapter 5, it is enough to say here that the work was a failure. Shortly after this disappointment, Hood and his wife suffered an incomparably harsher blow in the death of their first child soon after her birth. (The Hoods' chief comforters were Charles and Mary Lamb; one of Charles's best poems, "On an Infant Dying as Soon as Born," was prompted by this sad event.) Although distracted by grief and weakened by illness, Hood continued working without stint, determined not to be branded permanently as a jokester.

III *The Plea of the Midsummer Fairies*

The fiasco of *National Tales* seems only to have stiffened Hood's determination to create a successful work in the serious vein; and, before the year 1827 was out, in October, his *The Plea of the Midsummer Fairies, Hero and Leander, Lycus the Centaur, and Other Poems* was on the booksellers' shelves. Regrettably, most copies of the work remained there. The public, unaccustomed to a Hood clad in the robes of Shelley and Keats, was disappointed. The remark attributed to Hood that the unsold copies had to be bought by the author to save them from being used as butter-wrappers shows that Hood could jest about his miseries,[26] but it may be only a slight exaggeration of the truth. The book deserved a better fate.

Of the poems to be surveyed here,[27] the leading title work claims first place. "The Plea of the Midsummer Fairies," dedicated to Charles Lamb, contains 125 quasi-Spenserian stanzas with the final line in each stanza regularized to iambic pentameter. Its genre is the familiar one of fairy-allegory, and its story can be quickly told. The narrator finds himself in fairyland. Queen Titania appears with her "pretty crew" of "lively peers," but she is in pensive and not sportive mood. She laments that the fairies, though not subject to human mortality, must fade from existence when poets no longer make them live in men's imaginations. Her "dark misgivings" are confirmed by the appearance of dread Saturn, "King of Years," who is to wield his sickle on the fairy crew because he is tired of their singing and craves "some newer song." Not even the eloquence of Puck or Ariel can dissuade him. Just as the Titan prepares his deadly blow, "a timely apparition" (actually the shade of Shakespeare) intervenes for the fairies. Saturn swings his weapon at the spirit, through whom it passes harmlessly (the meaning is, of course, that immortal poets like Shakespeare are invulnerable to the passage of time). The "King of Years," numb with wrath and frustration, retreats to his "Cimmerian gloom." The spirit of Shakespeare has made the fairies live forever, and so must all poets do.

The chief literary influences on "The Plea" announce themselves plainly enough. The most pervasive of these is Keats's *Endymion,* or we might say Keats's poetry as a whole.[28] The Keatsian texture of the work is disclosed in the opening stanza:

> 'Twas in that mellow season of the year,
> When the hot Sun singes the yellow leaves
> Till they be gold,—and with a broader sphere
> The Moon looks down on Ceres and her sheaves;
> When more abundantly the spider weaves,
> And the cold wind breathes from a chillier clime;
> That forth I fared, on one of those still eves,
> Touch'd with the dewy sadness of the time,
> To think how the bright months had spent their prime.

Shakespeare's *A Midsummer Night's Dream* and, of course, Spenser's *The Faerie Queene* also left their marks on this poem, as perhaps did also Michael Drayton's "Nymphidia, the Court of Fairy" and John Lyly's *Endimion, or The Man in the Moon.*

Several good things can be said of "The Plea of the Midsummer Fairies." It has more than the common portion of winsome, antiquated charm characteristic of all good fairy tales; the language is, for the most part, tasteful as well as rich and colorful; the conceits are ingenious and ingratiating; the pacing is adroitly handled, in view of the great length of the story. Finally, the use of "bold Chanticleer" to announce the dawn and thus to disperse the fairies, although quite conventional, effects a pleasing and appropriate end to the poet's vision of the fairy folk.

On the other hand, it cannot be denied that "The Plea" has faults. In the first place, we are tempted to object, as Dr. Johnson did to Milton's "Lycidas," that there is "nothing new" in it. Hood occasionally equals his sources but seldom if ever surpasses them, and we feel that we have heard the poem before. Of course, this familiarity might make the poem more appealing to some readers, but even they would probably find it too long. As Agnes Repplier has remarked with not unkind asperity, "midsummer fairies had no business to plead for a hundred and twenty-six stanzas." [29] For another thing, "The Plea" does not always maintain the golden mean between elfin delicacy and euphuistic preciosity; it becomes, in Heath-Stubbs' phrase, "somewhat pretty-pretty." [30] We scarcely expect the vocabulary of an Ernest Hemingway in fairy-allegory, but to find "twittering race" and "feather'd throng" (11. 271, 276) in one stanza is really too much. "The pastoral cowslips are our little pets" (1. 316) and "Or glad thy fingers on his smooth soft skin" (1. 377) remind us, not agreeably, of Leigh Hunt; and "With wholesome texts learned from kind nature's books" (1. 665) seems a stale Wordsworthian titbit. Such lines are not numerous enough to spoil the poem (the agreeable quality of its language as a whole has been noted), but surely they contribute nothing to it.

All in all, it would be fair to describe "The Plea of the Midsummer Fairies" as a graceful, pleasing, but overlong fairy fantasy. Hood's audience, like his Saturn, were "weary for some newer song"; they had found it in his humorous verse and wanted more of this, not Keats and Spenser in patched-up garments. William Michael Rossetti, an admirer of Hood, spoke for both his age and ours when he said "*The Midsummer Fairies* was one of the author's own favourite works, and certainly deserved to be so, as far as dainty elegance of motive and of execution is concerned: but the conception was a little too ingeniously remote for the public to ratify the author's predilection." [31]

"Hero and Leander," Hood's version of the popular love story first told by Musaeus Grammaticus in the fifth century but known to most readers through the Elizabethan poem begun by Christopher Marlowe and finished by George Chapman, is a poem that has divided the critics. Rossetti lauded it as "a most astonishing example of revivalist poetry: it is reproductive and spontaneous at the same time. It resembles its models closely, not servilely—significantly, not mechanically." [32] George Saintsbury was more cautious but clearly favorable: "hardly shall anyone come off better in vying with Christopher Marlowe." [33] In our own century, Agnes Repplier has found "Hero and Leander" lacking in both narrative power and sentiment; [34] and Laurence Brander, while giving Hood credit for some originality, thinks that his poem is generally inferior to its Elizabethan prototype. [35] On the other hand, the poem has been praised by Douglas Bush and J. C. Reid, [36] who feel much as Rossetti did about it.

The stanzaic form of "Hero and Leander" recalls many Elizabethan poems, among them Shakespeare's *Venus and Adonis*: each stanza contains six iambic pentameter lines rhyming *ababcc*. Among its users in the Romantic period are Shelley ("Marenghi") and Keats ("To Hope"). "Hero and Leander" seems even more Keatsian than "The Plea of the Midsummer Fairies"; indeed, one collating the language and imagery of Hood's poem with *Endymion*'s must keep written lists to escape befuddlement. The kinship is not due primarily to similarities in the actual stories, although there are some: both poems include an undersea adventure, use of the mortal-immortal theme, and the myth of Scylla. Far more notable is the resemblance in language: Hood employs many words that are favorites of the Keats of 1816–18, a few being "pearly," "argent," "ooze" ("oozy," "ooz'd"), "bubbled" ("bubbles," "bubbling"), "crystal," "golden," "emerald," "sobbings," and "luxuries." Occasionally there are larger parallels. Scylla's plea to Leander in Hood's work (11. 379–426) makes us think of several impassioned speeches in *Endymion*, such as Alpheus' to Arethusa (II, 936 ff.), Circe's to Glaucus (III, 429 ff.), and Endymion's to the Indian Maid (IV, 622 ff.). Especially striking are the two poets' descriptions of the awesome sights beneath the ocean's depths.[37]

The best-known lyric in *The Plea of the Midsummer Fairies* after "Fair Ines" is "I Remember, I Remember." [38] These two poems are almost identical in stanzaic form, the only important difference being in the first line of each stanza, where "I Remember" has four trochees. Although only a full reading can do the poem justice, the tone and form of the whole are suggested by the final stanza:

> I remember, I remember,
> The fir trees dark and high;
> I used to think their slender tops
> Were close against the sky:
> It was a childish ignorance,
> But now 'tis little joy
> To know I'm farther off from heav'n
> Than when I was a boy.

This passage inevitably recalls Wordsworth's "poetry of memory," to use F. W. Bateson's phrase.[39] It is doubtful, though, that "I Remember" owes much, if anything, to Hood's reading of Wordsworth, despite the reminder of the great "Intimations Ode" in the closing lines. Certainly the rhythms are not Wordsworth's. Some of the word pictures recall the older poet's, but in no significant way: birds, flowers, pools, and trees were not the special property of William Wordsworth. Above all, there is a simplicity about Hood's poem: it is practically uncomplicated by philosophical reflection. Hood is not concerned to reconcile great opposites but simply to recall in nostalgic mood, as people commonly do, the pastoral charm of childhood after it has taken on a poignant, bittersweet quality by contrast with the cluttered harshness of the adult world. (We may note in passing that Hood does the same thing in a lighter vein in "A Retrospective Review," also in this volume.) The poet's *feeling* in "I Remember" is closer to that of Gray's "Ode on a Distant Prospect of Eton College" than to that of Wordsworth's masterpiece; but Hood's perspective is the opposite of Gray's.

Of the remaining lyrics in *The Plea of the Midsummer Fairies*, several are not lacking in merit; among these are "Song: 'The stars are with the voyager'"; "Ruth"; and "Autumn" ("The Autumn skies are flush'd with gold" [40]). None, however, bears close comparison with "Fair Ines" and "I Remember"; and, since these rich but delicate poems were lost in the whole, the volume on which Hood had staked his hopes as a serious poet was a failure. The public preferred the scintillating punster and parodist to the competent but generally rather bland disciple of Keats. Thomas Hood's independent lyrical talents were to be developed on different lines from those discernible in *The Plea of the Midsummer Fairies*. Readers of Hood will do well to ponder Reid's suggestion that this development might not have occurred had the book succeeded; [41] therefore, better a fortunate failure than an unfortunate success.

IV Whims and Oddities, Second Series; *Comedies;* The Gem

After the debacle of the work which Hood had hoped would rescue him from the label of "funny man," he was sufficiently a realist to return for the time to what was expected of him; and in October, 1827, he rushed through the press *Whims and Oddities, Second Series*. Like its namesake, this was a mélange of comic pieces in prose and verse. To enter into the book at length would be to allow disproportionate space to the types of humorous verse already noted in the first *Whims and Oddities* and in *Odes and Addresses to Great People*: the Byronic pastiche ("Bianca's Dream"), the lightweight satire ("The Progress of Art"), the "pathetic ballad" ("Mary's Ghost"), the jesting ode ("Ode to the Cameleopard"), and the gruesomely facetious tale ("The Demon-Ship"). Like its earlier companion, the 1827 *Whims and Oddities* pleased the public enormously; for once more it had the Hood that it knew and loved.

Hood had now fathered five volumes within a year, to say nothing of other publications; and his body—never very strong—finally failed his spirit. Nevertheless, he resumed work as energetically as ever following a brief holiday at Brighton late in 1827. He even tried his hand at playwrighting.[42] Hood's first attempt at drama had been made some years earlier—no one seems to know precisely when—with a play based on Keats's "Lamia." Probably this lusterless work was never intended for the stage; [43] the fact that Hood never tried to publish it might mean that he himself recognized its limitations.[44] In 1828, however, he was confident enough of his powers to attempt a work for the stage. The best known of Hood's dramatic efforts—the farce *York and Lancaster, or a School without Scholars*—was finally staged at the Adelphi Theatre about eight months after its composition; it was a mediocre production even by the uncritical standards of the London stage in the 1820's. There is reason to believe that Hood also contributed some songs to a musical comedy, *Mr. Sims;* but this work, like so many ephemera of its kind, has disappeared.[45] Furthermore, in the 1870 edition of Hood's *Whimsicalities* was published "Lost and Found. —A Fragment. A Farce"; possibly this work was part of one submitted for presentation at Drury Lane late in 1826 or early in 1827, but it is unlikely that the point can be definitely settled.[46] Even Thomas Hood's keenest admirers must find him a failure as a playwright, but it is possible that he need not have been. Whitley finds it "curious" that Hood so "consistently refused to employ his best talents" in his dramatic efforts, for his skill in blending humor and pathos might well have made him a popular writer of domestic comedy and melodrama.[47]

Hood was far more successful with his first annual, *The Gem,* which appeared under his editorship in 1828. At this time the annual or "gift book," practically a household fixture, had splendiferous covers that concealed a potpourri of mediocre to appalling sentimental verse and illustrations to match, redeemed partially and infrequently by a contribution of enduring worth. Doubtless it was the popularity of the annuals that inspired Huckleberry Finn's posthumous sketch of Emmeline Grangerford: it is noteworthy that one of the volumes in the Grangerfords' small but ponderous library was *"Friendship's Offering,* full of beautiful stuff and poetry" [48]—a volume to which Hood himself contributed.[49]

The Gem, several cuts above the average annual in literary content, boasted the works of Keats,[50] Lamb,[51] Scott, Clare, Reynolds, and Hartley Coleridge. Hood's major offering was "The Dream of Eugene Aram, the Murderer," still one of his most widely acclaimed poems.[52] Of the other poems that Hood wrote for *The Gem*—"The Farewell," "Birthday Verses," and "On a Picture of Hero and Leander"—the latter is of special interest because of his longer work on the same subject. The title suggests at once the Keatsian sonnet mentioned in note 50, but the tone of the poem is closer to that of Byron's "Written after Swimming from Sestos to Abydos." Actually, though, it is pure Hood: "Must a lad of *Greece*

/ Come all over *dripping?*" (11. 7–8). And this poem was written by the same man whose "Hero and Leander" has been called by a distinguished modern critic "probably the most remarkable example in modern verse of almost complete reproduction of the narrative manner of the Elizabethan Ovidians"! [53] Hood's variety is simply astonishing.

Because of the superior content and because of Hood's excellent editing, *The Gem* sold exceedingly well; and Hood was now firmly established as a successful poet, humorist, and journalist. Unfortunately, he lacked the sound business sense attributed to his father, or perhaps he was just more unfortunate than he deserved to be.[54] Whatever the reason, he resigned his editorship of *The Gem*, apparently because of disagreements with its publishers. Another instance of Hood's ill-fortune or bad judgment in business matters was his quitting the staff of the *Athenaeum*, a promising new journal that was to live up to its auspicious beginnings under the leadership of Charles Wentworth Dilke (now remembered mainly as a friends of Keats). It should be added that Hood continued to publish occasionally in the *Athenaeum* and to remain on very friendly terms with Dilke.

V   The Epping Hunt, *the* Comic Annual *Poems, and Others*

Hood's first work of consequence after his abandonment of *The Gem* was *The Epping Hunt*, published early in the fall of 1829 as a separate volume. Clearly inspired by William Cowper's "The Diverting History of John Gilpin," this equally diverting history tells of a stodgy London merchant who in an insane moment decides to "go society" in a red coat and to take part in the celebrated Epping Hunt. *The Epping Hunt* is notable chiefly for averaging more puns in each stanza than any poem of comparable length in the annals of poetry. The following examples are typical: "For this contained the *deer alive,* / And not the dear deceased!" (11. 203–4); "On horse and ass—like high and low / And Jack pursuing game!" (11. 223–24); "Now flew to 'hills we know not of,' / Now, nun-like, took the vale" (11. 271–72). (One of the best puns is not in the poem itself but in Hood's advertisement of the second or 1830 edition: "the *Lex Tallyho-nis,* or Laws of Hunting.")

In this work, as in most of Hood's comic tales, many of his devices and situations are familiar enough. For example, most of us have chuckled cruelly over the plight of an inept rider thrown from his mount into a cactus or thorn bush, but it is doubtful that we can recall an account to equal Hood's:

> Right glad was he, as well might be,
> Such cushion to resign:
> 'Possession is nine points,' but his
> Seemed more than ninety-nine.
>   (11. 353–56)

The Epping Hunt is enlivened by smile-provoking glances at Shakespeare's *Hamlet,* Gray's "Elegy Written in a Country Churchyard," Burns's "Tam O'Shanter," and Byron's "Mazeppa"; [55] and there is a sprinkling of facetious Classical allusions and harmless impieties.[56] All in all, the poem is exactly what Hood meant it to be—good fun and nothing more.

A far more more ambitious project than *The Epping Hunt* had been in the making since the last part of 1828, although it was not marketed until 1830. Capitalizing on the great popularity of the annuals, Hood, in a fortunate moment of inspiration, decided to put together a *Comic Annual* mostly from his own works—not only poems and prose sketches, but also engravings and drawings. (The latter must, of course, be seen to be appreciated.) This first *Comic Annual* included a few offerings from other writers, among them Reynolds, Horace Smith (the former friend of Shelley), and Keats.[57] An instant hit with the public, the work was so widely imitated that the comic annual soon became almost as common in British households as its more pretentious prototype. Hood was understandably irritated when the publishers of his *Comic Annual,* Hurst and Chance, brought out in 1831 the rival *New Comic Annual, or Falstaff's Annual* and actually used Hood's name to advertise it.[58] Hood seems to have had some ground for his increasing disenchantment with the world of publishers and printers, which became almost chronic: during its long life (1830–39, 1842), the *Comic Annual* had four different publishers. Hood's relationships with his readers certainly remained cordial enough, however; his son was to call the *Comic Annual* "the most popular of my Father's undertakings." [59] Never unambitious, Hood felt sure enough of his reputation to dedicate the 1832 *Annual* to King William IV. This act earned him the favor of a royal audience, which Hood made memorable in the best funny-man tradition by backing from his monarch's presence into the wrong doorway.[60]

Since the history of the *Comic Annuals* spans a good many years, it would be well to have in mind some of the events of the author's life during this period before examining specimens of the poetry from these volumes. A glance at the "Chronology" shows that this period was a harrowing and hectic one for the Hoods. The ill fortune that haunted Hood in his business dealings was not abated; rather, it worsened. To what extent Hood was responsible is arguable, but he certainly showed bad judgment at times, as when he moved his family to the impractical and pretentious Lake House in Essex; and he justified the move (as people do) by saying that he would make it profitable by farming the acreage—"he who scarcely knew grass-seed from gunpowder." [61] Hood's dream of becoming a gentleman farmer was just that, but his sojourn at Lake House did help to inspire the creation of *Tylney Hall* (1834), the full-length serious novel that Hood had long yearned to produce.

Although successful, this work demanded such a greedy share of the author's time and energy that it really brought him more loss than gain. Hood's financial situation went from critical to desperate and thence to disastrous; finally, in March, 1835, he fled alone to the Continent to escape the hounding of creditors and to attempt a financial comeback without fear of interruption. Later he was joined by his family, and the Hoods' uneasy "visit" in Germany and Belgium did not end until the spring of 1840. As we browse through Hood's *Comic Annuals,* we must remember that several of the items were prepared while he was in exile and in anything but a comic mood (although his sense of humor was never wholly lost).

It would be impracticable to attempt even a superficial inspection of all the poems in the *Comic Annuals* (many of which appeared first in various magazines); indeed, few show sufficient variation from the specimens of Hood's verse already considered to justify such a survey. We notice at once the familiar types: light, playful, usually charming things like "I'm Not a Single Man" (1831), "The Cigar" (1833), "The Bachelor's Dream" (1839), and "The Vision" (1839); mock odes like the "Ode to Joseph Hume, Esq., M.P." (1832); [62] satires, mostly light, like "A Public Dinner" (1833), "A Charity Sermon" (1833), "Drinking Song by a

Member of the Temperance Society" (1837), "Agricultural Distress" (1837), "Hit or Miss" (1838), "A Plain Direction" (1839), "The Doctor" (1839), "An Open Question" (1842), and "A Tale of a Trumpet" (1842).

A few words must be said, however, about some of the satiric pieces such as [63] "Hit or Miss," which, inspired in part by Robert Burns's "The Twa Dogs"—a brief quotation from which precedes the poem—is a long, engagingly written dialogue between a pointer and a spaniel which not so incidentally satirizes their human masters and all their kind, especially hunters. It is a kind of verbal equivalent of a present-day animated cartoon. "A Plain Direction" and "The Doctor" make telling use of ironic refrain. In the first of these an *ingénu* traveler, ever searching for a utopia free from poverty, hypocrisy, and political corruption, is assured at the close of every stanza that his way lies "Straight down the Crooked Lane, / And all round the Square." In the second poem, Hood's doctor—surely a descendant of the one described by Swift in Book IV of *Gulliver's Travels*—has one invariable answer when told of the consequences of his prescription (even when it is death): "'Yes, yes,' said the Doctor, / 'I meant it for that!'" Although needlessly long (812 lines), "A Tale of a Trumpet" is a well-told story of a deaf old lady who acquires a miraculous ear-trumpet through which she hears all the scandal and gossip in her community. Hood shows a Burnsian or Byronic perspicacity in stripping moral hypocrisy of its sanctimonious trappings. He could not, of course, foresee the unsettling effect of the poem on today's reader, for whom the trumpet seems ominously prophetic of the mail-order electronic detector.

Several interesting poems in the *Comic Annuals* do not fit well into any of the categories mentioned earlier. One of these, "On the Death of Sir Walter Scott" (1833), is cited in its entirety:

> Farewell, Sir Walter Scott, secured
> From Time,—our greatest of Inditers!
> No Author's fame so well *assur'd*,
> For all who wrote were *Under-writers*.

Hood, most inveterate and inventive of punsters, has dared much indeed; and some readers will be offended. But others, probably the majority, will not find the epitaph in bad taste (although they might wish that Hood had omitted the italics). Who but Hood could turn a pun on a deceased colleague into a splendid tribute?

A more substantial work is the "Ode for St. Cecilia's Eve" (1831). As the title suggests, this is a parody of John Dryden's "Alexander's Feast or The Power of Music; an Ode in Honor of St. Cecilia's Day: 1697." Considering the length and complexity of the original, we should hardly be going too far to call this Hood poem one of the outstanding parodies in English verse. A hilarious address to a group of musicians whose courting of the Muse rivals that of Peter Quince and Company in *A Midsummer Night's Dream*, Hood's very free imitation of Dryden's majestic ode can be appreciated only by reading the two poems successively. Here there is room only for Hood's closing lines, which immediately recall Dryden's ("He rais'd a mortal to the skies; / She drew an angel down"):

> O Music! praises thou hast had,
>   From Dryden and from Pope,
> For thy good notes, yet none I hope,
>   But I, e'er praised the bad,
> Yet are not saint and sinner even?
> Miss Strummel on Cecilia's level?
> One drew an angel down from heaven!
> The other scar'd away the devil!

Another *Comic Annual* poem, "The Blue Boar" (1837), is remembered mainly because it triggered the composition of one of Hood's best satires. Mr. Rae Wilson, a Scottish globe-trotter who nourished his vanity by writing mediocre travel books that his wealth enabled him to have printed, had on several occasions attacked Hood's work as immoral and as irreverent. When Wilson made some harmless lines in "The Blue Boar" the ground for a special attack, Hood, unable to ignore Wilson's clumsy sniping any longer, published in the *Athenaeum* his devastating "Ode to Rae Wilson, Esq." Like Burns's great "Holy Willie's Prayer," this work not only pins a pious bigot squirming to the board but stands as a timeless indictment of his kind. The "Ode to Rae Wilson" is important also for its partial revelation of Hood's personal religious feelings, especially since his abhorrence of blatant piety usually made him very reticent on this subject. As Hood's son was to say after the poet's death, "My father's religious faith was deep and sincere: but it was but little known to a world ever apt to decide by hearing professions, rather than by scrutinising actions." [64] After this observation, the following lines from "Ode to Rae Wilson" need no comment:

> A man may cry 'Church! Church!' at ev'ry word,
> With no more piety than other people—
> A daw's not reckoned a religious bird
> Because it keeps a-cawing from a steeple.
> The Temple is a good, a holy place,
> But quacking only gives it an ill savour;
> While saintly mountebanks the porch disgrace,
> And bring religion's self into disfavour!
>
> (ll. 171–78)

A special place of honor has been reserved for the *magnum opus* of the *Comic Annuals*: "Miss Kilmansegg and Her Precious Leg" (1842).[65] For this tale of 2,389 lines, Hood rivaled Lord Byron in his selection of a verse form admirably suited to sustained humorous narrative. The stanzas are mostly of six or seven lines, occasionally of eight and rarely of nine or more, with tetrameters predominating over trimeters by about seven to three; sometimes there is a bouncy run of dimeters, as in the middle stanzas of the section subtitled "Her Birth." (The poem has seventeen such sections, including the very brief concluding one, "Her Moral.") As Pritchett says, if the "plot groans," at least the "lines scamper." [66]

Baldly epitomized, the plot of "Miss Kilsmansegg" seems trivial and grotesque. The heroine, only child of a family whose wealth is equaled only by its vulgarity, acquires her "precious leg" of gold to replace the natural one lost in a hunting accident. The new limb creates a sensation: Miss Kilmansegg is envied by all and courted by many. She chooses as her husband a worthless, depraved Continental nobleman who clubs his wife to death with the golden leg and runs away with it—and so ends the story! Surprisingly, when read in its entirety, "Miss Kilmansegg" is found to be a really brilliant imaginative work; we might even legitimately ask whether it is equaled in its genre within the whole corpus of nineteenth-century English poetry. If Byron's *Don Juan* is the epic of modern life, "Miss Kilsmansegg" may claim to be its epyllion. Although very long, the poem is not tiresome, except perhaps occasionally when the incorrigible pun-maker Hood lapses into a "groaner" like *"Hairess"* or *"pursy-verance."* [67]

Some of Hood's best word-plays, punnic and other, are in this work. In the first place, the myriad references to gold or words suggesting gold ("auriferous"), and particularly the repetition of "Gold! and gold!" (or variations on this phrase), not only sustain thematic unity but also become an insistent commentary on the values of modern society. Among the countless *bons mots* in "Miss Kilmansegg," the following deserve notice: [68]

> It wouldn't require much verbal strain
> To trace the Kill-man, perchance, to Cain;
> (11. 8–9)

> The Leg! the Leg! was the great event,
> Through every circle of life it went,
>   Like the leg of a pair of compasses.
> (11. 856–58)

> The page, who looked so splendidly clad,
> Like a page of the 'Wealth of Nations.'
> (11. 1589–90)

"Miss Kilmansegg" may, of course, be regarded as a satire on money snobbery, but some portions stand out as gems of social satire on particular matters. One of these reminds us that fads change only slightly, while the people enslaved by them change not at all:

> The Golden Leg had a vast career,
> It was sung and danced—and to show how near
>   Low Folly to lofty approaches,
> Down to society's very dregs,
> The Belles of Wapping wore 'Kilmanseggs,'
> And St. Giles's Beaux sported Golden Legs
>   In their pinchbeck pins and brooches.
> (11. 895–901)

Hood also takes some quasi-Byronic flings at upper-class marriages: [69]

> For next to that interesting job,
> The hanging of Jack, or Bill, or Bob,
> There's nothing so draws a London mob
> As the noosing of very rich people.
>   (11. 1573–76)

There is some out-and-out political satire in the poem, as when it relates that the heroine "stood on a Member that cost as much / As a Member for all the County!" (11. 822–23). The most devastating passage in this vein, regrettably too long to quote, is the one on the "Evil Spirit of Party" that opens "Her Fancy Ball" (11. 944–66). Sometimes the author indicts both the social and the political structures of his day in words that remind us of the "protest" poems studied in Chapter 6. After mentioning the unfortunate lot of poor girls, he assures us that it was

> Not so with the infant Kilmansegg!
> She was not born to steal or beg,
>   Or gather cresses in ditches;
> To plait the straw or bind the shoe,
> Or sit all day to hem and sew,
> As females must, and not a few—
>   To fill their insides with stitches!
>
> She was not doom'd for bread to eat
> To be put to her hands as well as her feet—
>   To carry home linen from mangles—
> Or heavy-hearted, and weary-limb'd,
> To dance on a rope in a jacket trimm'd
>   With as many blows as spangles.
>   (11. 119–31) [70]

Such lines help us remember that the author of this brilliant but sometimes gruesome semi-allegorical fantasy is the same Hood who wrote such a direct and moving poem as "The Song of the Shirt."

Practically all the qualities for which Hood is best known are displayed in "Miss Kilmansegg and Her Precious Leg": whimsy, satire, double-entendre, the humorous-macabre, and even social protest. About the only thing missing is tender domestic sentiment, and even it is present by implication; a man who can aim such shattering blasts at the perversion of love and virtue must harbor tender feelings toward the real thing. With "Miss Kilmansegg" Hood has attained complete maturity, though not yet complete fulfillment, as a poet.

Two other publications in the subject area of this chapter must be briefly dealt with. One of these, *Hood's Own*, was—with the major exception of the "Literary Reminiscences" and a few minor ones—a republication in periodical form of items already successfully issued in, for the most part, the *Comic Annuals*. Launched in January, 1838, *Hood's Own* ran for thirteen numbers before being published as a separate volume in 1839; and it was received enthusiastically in both forms. Equally popular was *Whimsicalities*, which appeared in two volumes late in 1843 (dated 1844). The bulk of this work is in prose, and of the poems few are either novel or meritorious enough to claim a hearing. It would be unfair, however, to suppress altogether the clever epigrams that grace its pages here and there, like "On Lieutenant Eyre's Narrative of the Disasters at Cabul":

> A sorry tale of sorry plans,
> Which this conclusion grants,
> That Afghan clans had all the *Khans*
> And we had all the can'ts.

or the one entitled simply "Epigram":

> Three traitors, Oxford—Francis—Bean,
> Have missed their wicked aim;
> And may all shots against the Queen,
> In future do the same:
> For why, I mean no turn of wit,
> But seriously insist
> That if Her Majesty were *hit*
> No one would be so *miss'd*.

As witty in its way, and of more enduring appeal, is the delightful simplicity of "The Season"; here is the third of its five stanzas:

> Round the tops of houses,
> Swallows, as they flit,
> Give, like yearly tenants,
> Notices to quit.

This chapter has viewed Hood's climb to the heights as a humorous writer, a career which proceeded rather steadily from his first professional publications to the triumph of the *Comic Annuals.* But we must be aware of the irony in using the word "success" to describe Hood's career. Especially from 1832 on, he was chronically ill and under continual harassment by creditors.[71] The profits from his best-selling works were either swallowed up by the abyss of debt or tied up by the hopeless tangle of litigation with publishers. Fortunately, Hood had two great resources to sustain him: a stubborn sense of humor and a loyal and sensible wife. Hood's situation seemed to improve with his appointment as editor of the *New Monthly Magazine* in August, 1841, a post which he filled with distinction; but again his cloud followed him. Unable for reasons of personal integrity to comply with what amounted to orders from his publisher to write "puffs" (flattering reviews of works by mediocre but influential authors), Hood resigned in the fall of 1843. In spite of his reputation as a writer and the friendship of eminent men and patrons of letters, including Dickens, Hood could not find an empty editorial chair. Steering the same course as that of the legendary discharged professor who founded his own school, early in 1844 Hood began his own journal, *Hood's Monthly Magazine and Comic Miscellany.* The fortunes of this periodical and an account of the best-remembered works appearing in it—works very different from those that had earned a precarious livelihood for a lively Hood—comprise a story belonging mainly to chapters 4 and 6.[72]

In these works we find a facet of Hood's talent thus far given only cursory mention: his propensity for the strange and macabre.

CHAPTER 4

The Macabre and the Grotesque

I *Introduction*

THOMAS Hood's attraction to the macabre and the *outré* has been glimpsed in several works mentioned in this study: "Faithless Sally Brown," "Faithless Nelly Gray,' "'The Doctor," and, of course, "Miss Kilmansegg." Because this element is so often treated lightly and good-humoredly or is subordinated to other concerns, we might read far into the Oxford Edition of Hood's poetry without noting the pervasiveness of the dark and lurid; like most of the author's contemporaries, we would visualize him as a master of light verse. Quite a contrary impression would be formed by beginning our study of Hood with "The Dream of Eugene Aram" or "The Haunted House."

Although this study is not a psychological one of Hood, some facts of his life that might have streaked his nature with morbidity may be briefly noted. First, death was a frequent visitor in Hood's family: at the age of twelve, he lost his father and his brother James; at twenty-two, his mother; at twenty-eight, his first child; and at thirty-two, his sister Anne. Probably more important is the fact that, from the age of sixteen, Hood was never really well. It is doubtful that any chronically ill person, however he may strive for balance, can entirely suppress a tendency toward what is tritely (though here literally) called "morbid curiosity." Would Robert Louis Stevenson have written his splendid "Aes Triplex" had he been as robust as a blacksmith? Edgar Allan Poe, no stranger to pain and weakness, gained from his own suffering the insight to say of Hood that "his peculiar genius was the result of vivid *Fancy* impelled by Hypochondriasis." [1]

On the other hand, it would be wrong to press the point just made without taking a closer look at the literary work of many of Hood's contemporaries—Thomas Rowlandson, George Cruik-shank, Richard Dagley, Francis Douce,[2] Thomas L. Beddoes, George Darley, Winthrop M. Praed, and even such notables as Charles Dickens and W. M. Thackeray (to say nothing of later

Victorians such as Walter Pater and others). All of these writers show at times a predilection toward the strange, the morbid, even the gruesome. Hood was by no means a solitary, sickly figure: his work reflects not only his own temperament but a kind of *mal du siècle* that seems to have affected all European literature following the exhaustion of High Romanticism.

Because so many of Hood's poems bear a touch, but no more than that, of the macabre or the peculiar, the problem of classification is uncommonly hard. Any such attempt must perforce be subjective, especially in borderline cases, and thus seemingly arbitrary. Clearly, not every work involving pain, sadness, or death falls into the group to be scanned here. "The Bridge of Sighs," for example, does not because its morbid character derived from an actual event on which Hood wrote to awaken public conscience. The touchstone used in this chapter will be the existence in a given poem of preoccupation with the morbid or grotesque at least partly for its own sake. These words are admittedly protean; but, after all, some terms must be used; and subjective responses can never be altogether avoided (nor should they). By the rationale just stated, 87 of the 431 poems that we can reasonably be sure are Hood's—fully one-fifth—belong in the category of the macabre and the grotesque. This number includes many of Hood's most famous works, among them "Miss Kilmansegg," "The Dream of Eugene Aram," "The Haunted House," and "The Last Man." Seventy-four belong to the genre that will be called *(faute de mieux)* the humorous-macabre (although humorous-grotesque would sometimes be more apropos); thirteen show a serious treatment of the morbid or preternatural. Only a handful of these can be investigated at any length; those selected are, however, the ones most representative of Hood's practice.

II   *The Humorous-Macabre and Humorous-Grotesque*

It was just remarked that most of the poems by Hood showing a morbid bent are in a more or less comic vein. Even his punning, a device which we normally consider rather facilely comic, often has something of a "sick" quality; perhaps Poe was not far wrong when he said of Hood's puns that "far too evidently they are the hypochondriac's struggles at mirth—the grinning of the death's head." [3] Certainly, this statement is not always applicable to Hood's sparkling word-plays. It might well be true, though, as

Reid suggests,[4] that, when the habit of punning is so persistent as it is in Hood, it bespeaks a basic duality in the writer's view of life. To speak metaphorically, one whose existence is somewhat like a tightrope dance without a net will be forced to become so familiar with the constant threat of pain and danger that, to make his life at all tolerable, he must accept the tragic in the commonplace and the ridiculous and must see these, in turn, as other than what they seem.

Something similar could be said of Hood's incorrigible fondness for practical jokes.[5] The lovers of this dubious form of humor surely have varying motives, but it may be theorized that behind most of them is a sense of frustration, the causes of which may be legion but the result of which is usually a resentment, bitterness, or even malice that eventually demands satisfaction from the world. It is this fact that makes it possible for Whipple to say, shortly after stressing Hood's "genial kindness" and "humanity," that "Indeed, there is occasionally a little misanthropy in him." [6] Through practical joking, the sufferer can relieve his feelings in a comparatively harmless way: the practice is not laudable, but its results are generally innocuous when weighed against the possibility of violence or psychosis. It is easy to see that the poetry by Hood under focus here contains an immense amount of vicarious practical joking; and we suspect at times that behind this clown's mask is a countenance ravaged by bitterness—a bitterness that neither Hood's discretion nor his humanity would allow him to express fully and directly.

The plight of Hood just described is in some measure that of nearly all men, as is evidenced by the frequency with which the painful, brutal, and terrible are given comic treatment. This phenomenon appears throughout practically the entire range of literature: from the ancient mock-epic *Batrachomyomachia* through Aristophanes and the whole history of sophisticated comedy; in Shakespeare pre-eminently; in Swift's *A Modest Proposal* (the *ne plus ultra* of its genre); in the shipwreck and war cantos of Byron's *Don Juan;* in a host of miscellaneous authors and works that come trooping in for their share of notice—Poe's "The Man That Was Used Up" and "Hop-Frog," the operas of Gilbert and Sullivan, the stories of Stephen Crane, and scores of others. The popularity of an oxymoronic blending of laughter and tears in folk culture is witnessed by perennial folk-song favorites like "Peter

Gray," "The Bold Fisherman," and "The Unfortunate Man." Finally, we need not be reminded of the near-mania for so-called "sick humor" in our day. The phase of cultural history just glanced at cannot be explained away as deliberate cultivation of the unexpected or of the improper for the sake of humorous incongruity or dramatic irony. At a deeper level, the purpose might be to relieve feelings of defeat, bafflement, hostility, and fear by making the dreadful common and ridiculous.

A few generalizations can be made about the form and content of Hood's lighter grotesqueries. Of special types, there are only three that appear more than once or twice. By far the commonest is the ballad, which frequently bears the subtitle "A Pathetic Ballad" or something similar; among the fourteen examples of this genre are such comparative masterpieces as "Mary's Ghost," "John Day," "Sally Simpkin's Lament," "The Poacher," and "Ben Bluff," besides those mentioned earlier. Four are epitaphs, elegies, or laments: "Elegy on David Laing, Esq.," "On a Royal Demise," "The Lament of Toby, the Learned Pig," and "A Lament for the Decline of Chivalry." Finally, there are four mock-odes—to "Mr. Malthus," "Dr. Hahnemann," "H. Bodkin, Esq.," and "Spencer Perceval."

Hood's favorite subjects in the realm of the comically grotesque, which often overlap, are ghosts and apparitions (nine poems), the sea (eight poems), the military (five poems), and dreams (four poems). So summary a statement gives but a faint idea, however, of Hood's variety. We find a whaleman who makes a somnambulistic effort to harpoon his rather cetacean wife ("Ben Bluff"), a toper who passes out near the dyer's and awakens with a half-green face ("The Green Man"), a sausage-maker who goes through his own machine ("The Sausage-Maker's Ghost"), a frustrated porcine Oxonian ("The Lament of Toby"), a "dead beat" who must pay his overdue medical bill or have his severed nose sewed on upside down ("A True Story")—and many more such fantastic characters and situations.

The most unforgettable examples of Hood's bizarre comedy are those dominated by the ghastly and gruesome—in a word, by horror. This penchant of Hood's is seen early in his work, as in his lines on the one-armed beggar in "Ode to H. Bodkin, Esq." (1825) (the key word is italicized):

> Poor Jack is gone, that used to doff
> His batter'd tatter'd hat,

> And show his dangling sleeve, alas!
> There seem'd no *arm* in that!
> (11. 33–36)

This rollicking ghastliness, if the phrase be allowed, is seen especially in the ballads. "Sally Simpkin's Lament" (1829), for example, is a dialogue between a maiden and the ghost of her lover, whose legs were removed by a shark:

> 'Oh! Sally, sharks do things by halves,
> Yet most completely do!
> A bite in one place seems enough,
> But I've been bit in two.
> (11. 13–16)

In another ballad, "The Supper Superstition" (1839), a sailor's ghost warns his family not to finish a sea-food dinner lest his kinfolk commit cannibalism—for the fish have ingested his remains.

A little of this sort of thing goes a long way, and not all readers find Hood's cleverness sufficient recompense for his occasional preoccupation with the physically horrible. Some might sense a gleeful cruelty in his description of an aching tooth in "A True Story" (1827):

> It had an universal sting;
> One touch of that extatic [7] stump
> Could jerk his limbs, and make him jump,
> Just like a puppet on a string.
> (11. 29–32)

Is this the sadism of a near-invalid resentful of all healthy people, or does Hood sport with suffering to make his own easier to bear? Again, these lines from "Pompey's Ghost" (1840) might be found very funny or simply distasteful:

> At last I got so sick of life,
> And sick of being dosed,
> On Monday morning I gave up
> My physic and the ghost!
> (11. 69–72)

We shall never be able to determine to what extent Hood's own medical history was responsible for his fascination with pathology, although it is significant that, as will be seen, his personal illness is the subject of some of his humorous verse. On one point, at least, there is general agreement: passages like those cited above are certainly effective. The lines on toothache can make us jump with the figurative puppet; the play on numbers in "Sally Simpkin's Lament" and the outrageous zeugma in "Pompey's Ghost" force a smile, though possibly a distorted one. Sometimes Hood achieves a genuine imaginative élan, as when he has his legless sailor say

> 'One half is here, the other half
>   Is near Columbia placed;
> Oh! Sally, I have got the whole
>   Atlantic for my waist.
>   (ll. 33–36)

Present-day readers, nurtured on cinematic and televised "realism" and "sick" humor are not likely to object so strenuously as some of Hood's Victorian readers did to his treatment of death. Hood no longer needs anyone to defend him by saying that his "wit plays about the tomb somewhat daringly, but still he can hardly be said to disturb its sanctities." [8] Most twentieth-century readers find wholly entertaining the poem "Epicurean Reminiscences of a Sentimentalist" (1839), a monologue by a bereaved husband whose every memory, however sorrowful, is overshadowed by the recollection of gustatory delights:

> For months still I linger'd in hope and in doubt,
>   While her form it grew wasted and thin;
> But the last dying spark of existence went out
>   As the oysters were just coming in!
>   (ll. 49–52)

Even modern readers might be slightly unsettled, as they must surely be entertained, by the "Ode to Mr. Malthus" (1839). In this rather Swiftian piece, a distracted father of fifteen children records his thoughts while reading Thomas Robert Malthus' *An Essay on the Principle of Population* (1798).[9] (It will be recalled that Malthus, contending that the birthrate would always overrun the food supply, recognized war and disease as necessary checks on population; in the revised edition, he also advocated "moral restraint.") Hood's narrator instantly finds himself a Malthusian. It would be a fine idea, he says, if, when the children crowd into Saint Paul's on Charity Day,

> ... the Bishop, then to make
> In this poor overcrowded world more room,
> Proposed to shake
> Down that immense extinguisher, the dome—
> (11. 101–4)

The proposal is horrifying, but so is the one that Swift called "Modest." Whether Hood's purpose is similar to Swift's, whether he is making a humorous and possibly satirical comment on the Malthusian theory, or whether he is exposing a momentary fit of misanthropy must be decided by the individual reader. In any case, the ingenuity of Hood's conceit must once more be acknowledged, although the comparison of the dome to a giant candle extinguisher is harder to appreciate now than it was in his time.[10]

A favorite device of Hood in dealing with the mock-terrible is bathos. Sometimes this contrivance gives a ridiculous turn to a passage that, if played straight, might be as evocative of horror and terror as "The Haunted House" or "The Dream of Eugene Aram." A work making frequent use of bathos is "The Forge: A Romance of the Iron Age" (1844); one example is found in the first stanza of this pseudo-Goethean fantasia:

> Like a dead man gone to his shroud,
> The sun has sunk in a coppery cloud,
> And the wind is rising squally and loud
>   With many a stormy token,—
> Playing a wild funereal air,
> Through the branches bleak, bereaved and bare,
> To the dead leaves dancing here and there—
>   In short, if the truth were spoken,
> It's an ugly night for anywhere,
>   But an awful one for the Brocken!

The casual, conversational "In short" deflates the entire passage and makes the reader wonder what kind of poem he has encountered. (Hood could have learned this trick from Byron.) Sometimes the two Hoods, the rib-tickler and the spine-tingler, are extremely close together, as in the fifth stanza (11. 37–46) of this same poem. Although a complete reading shows the closing lines to be bathetic, we might find the idea of mourning demons in itself strangely perturbing. Hood's tendency to dodge in and out of the penumbra between comedy and terror or tragedy is seen also in some of the poems of social protest (to which a later chapter is devoted).

Occasionally, Hood uses bathos on "the grand scale," notably in tales projected through a dream, a vision, or an hallucination: "The Last Man" (1826), "The Demon-Ship" (1827), "The Fall" (1832), and "The Desert-Born" (1837). In "The Demon-Ship," a shipwrecked sailor is thrown into an agony of terror when picked up by a sable ship with a black-visaged crew: surely he is "in the Devil's Ship, upon the Devil's Sea!" (1. 66). The sooty captain and his crew erupt in half-demented laughter: "A dozen gloomy shapes at once enjoy'd the merry fit, / With shriek and yell, and oaths as well, like Demons of the Pit" (11. 71–72). But ship and crew are black with nothing more frightening than honest coal dust, for the *Mary Ann of Shields* is a collier. Somehow, though, the air of infernal dread that has been so carefully developed in the poem survives its comic denouement. Anyone who has gone through a terrifying ordeal that has turned out to be harmless recognizes the psychological truth in Hood's creation: the recollection of such an experience is likely to be far more evocative of the terror than of the relief. Generally, these remarks apply also to "The Fall," the truly harrowing account of an unlucky canoeist who is swept over Niagara Falls and "dashed from ledge to ledge, / From crag to crag" (11. 24–25)[11]—until, at the very end, the spell is broken by a voice exclaiming "I declares! / He's been a-walking in his sleep, and pitch'd down all the stairs!" (11. 31–32). It is possible to see "The Fall" as a subconscious projection of the author's life—a continual averting of disaster through an ironic realization of his situation and a keen sense of the ridiculous.

"The Desert-Born" tells of an artist sketching in the Lebanese wilds who is chosen by a beautiful but sinister tribal queen to receive "the rarest gift of earth." But the queen's gift, like Juno's in the story of Cleobis and Biton, is a fearful thing: it is not the Circassian or Georgian charmer of the artist's fancy but a savage Arabian mare. Bound "Mazeppa-like, upon the Desert-Born" (1. 163), the victim has a wild ride that ends with "hideous shock" as his mount fails to clear a huge boulder. Luckily, though, the artist was not really on the mare's back but had "the NIGHT MARE on his chest" (1. 217).

The final poem to be considered in this group combining humor with the morbid or grotesque is "The Last Man" (1826). By far the grimmest of the lot, it is placed here rather than in the section following because of its use of a quasi-Surrealistic, half-infernal, and half-crazy humor that is wonderfully suited to the setting. The title of this strange poem is familiar through Thomas Campbell's poem (1812) and Mary Shelley's novel (1826); readers who know all three works might well agree with Heath-Stubbs that Hood's version passes both of these in lasting effect.[12] "The Last Man" also stirs memories of Byron's "Darkness" and Coleridge's "The Rime of the Ancient Mariner." We notice at once that Hood's stanza is precisely that of the eleven six-line stanzas in the latter poem—used also, as we have seen, in Hood's parody of Coleridge's masterpiece, "The Sea-Spell," [13] published with "The Last Man" in *Whims and Oddities, First Series.*

In Hood's simple story, the narrator, supposing himself to be the last survivor of a universal plague, suddenly discovers one other—a ragged, raffishly merry old beggar who shares his mouldy rations and proposes companionship. Disgusted by such a comrade, the protagonist soon leaves him for a spree of looting and decks himself out in aristocratic finery. When he finds the jolly old beggar doing the same, he is infuriated and hangs the offender. Then the murderer is suddenly staggered by the enormity of his deed: he has killed not just a filthy old ragamuffin but half the population of the globe! In an agony of remorse, the Last Man cuts the body down to bury it; but he is forced to give it to a pack of wild dogs who quickly tear the corpse into bloody shreds. Left in the unspeakably awful loneliness of a dead world, with no possible relief from hellish memory, the Last Man looks longingly at the scaffold:

> . . . but, alas! in vain
> My desperate fancy begs,—
> I must turn my cup of sorrows quite up,
> And drink it to the dregs,—
> For there is not another man alive,
> In the world, to pull my legs!
>   (11. 217–22)

On this note the tale ends. Hideous bathos can surely go no farther; and, for some readers, it might spoil the poem. Yet the conclusion is both artistically and psychologically sound. To turn the story into a suicide note at the end or to have the Last Man become a lunatic would be to court banality; certainly it would lessen the horrific impact that Hood has labored to produce. What possible ending is left, then? What, indeed, except the wild, despairing laughter that must be heard in Hell? If, as some suspect,[14] "The Last Man" is Hood's apocalypse of his world, we can be thankful that his spirit was not always dominated by the mood of this poem.

A few comic-macabre works are patently autobiographical. One, "Symptoms of Ossification" (1839), is a relatively light piece in which the poet declares "I fear my heart is ossifying!" because he can no longer weep over the fate of Goethe's Werther or thrill to Mrs. Siddons' roles. The theme is related to Byron's complaints in works so various as "Stanzas for Music" ("There's not a joy"), *Childe Harold's Pilgrimage*, III, iii–v, and *Don Juan*, IV, ii–iv. More painful, yet jaunty enough, is "A Few Lines on Completing Forty-Seven" (1839)—which, incidentally, Hood never did (he died about six years later, one year short of this mark). The final stanza projects the whimsy, pathos, and restraint of the poem:

> And when my body's turn'd to clay,
> And dear friends hear my knell,
> Oh, let them give a sigh and say—
> I hear the upstairs bell.

The last example to be given here, "Fragment: Probably Written During Illness" (of uncertain date but doubtless quite late), though hardly a masterpiece, shows through its telling use of repetition and the *bon mot* in the closing line that Hood has lost neither his sense of humor nor his facility in versification. Personal—and whimsical—though it is, this forlorn little piece speaks the timeless complaint of the chronically ill:

> I'm sick of gruel, and the dietetics,
> I'm sick of pills, and sicker of emetics,
> I'm sick of pulses' tardiness or quickness,
> I'm sick of blood, its thinness or its thickness,—
> In short, within a word, I'm sick of sickness!

III   Serious Poems of Darkness and Terror before 1829

Hood's really serious excursions across the frontiers of the tenebrous and terrible produced some of his best poems, such as "The Dream of Eugene Aram" and "The Haunted House." As might be expected, his earliest efforts in this kind were modest enough; the first worth mentioning is the Petrarchan sonnet "Midnight," published in the *London Magazine* in December, 1822. Night held a special attraction for the Romantics, and an interesting anthology of poems and excerpts on the subject could be compiled from their writings. Hood's "Midnight" would deserve a place in the collection, perhaps near Shelley's "To Night" and Keats's "To Sleep," both of which it somewhat resembles. Hood and Shelley see night as a dark, majestic spirit sweeping silently over the world; all three poets compare sleep to the effect of an anodyne; and all see a kinship between death and night.[15]

A considerably more ambitious effort than "Midnight" appeared five years later with the publication of Hood's "Ode to Melancholy" in *The Plea of the Midsummer Fairies* (1827). Although transparently suggested by Keats's "Ode on Melancholy," [16] the compression of Keats is utterly lacking: Hood's poem is, at 122 lines, just a shade over four times as long as Keats's. The stanzas are of irregular length, ranging from twelve to twenty-two lines, mainly tetrameters with occasional trimeters; the lines rhyme alternately or (infrequently) in couplets. As the first stanza will illustrate, the Keatsian element in "Ode to Melancholy" is so evident as to be almost oppressive:

> Come, let us set our careful breasts
> Like Philomel, against the thorn,
> To aggravate the inward grief,
> That makes her accents so forlorn;
> The world has many cruel points,
> Whereby our bosoms have been torn,
> And there are dainty themes of grief,
> In sadness to outlast the morn,—

Hood seems to be saying, as Keats does in the opening lines of "Ode on Melancholy," that we should not seek to stifle our darker moods but should rather nourish them in order to kindle syncretic insight. Keats, however, projects the idea through a careful and sensitive clustering of images; Hood has a tendency to fall back upon trite and vaporous abstraction. The phrase "dainty themes of grief" stirs a suspicion that the style of the poem is closer to that of *Endymion* and its predecessors than to that of the great odes, and a full reading confirms this feeling. Again we feel the force of Reid's statement that the lukewarm reception given *The Plea of the Midsummer Fairies* might have helped save Hood from becoming an inferior Keats.[17]

The least truly Keatsian lines in Hood's ode are those in which the author, like an eighteenth-century "graveyard poet" *redivivus,* dwells upon the funereal for its own sake. Keats often shows a preoccupation with death, especially in poems written after late 1818; but he is not so obvious nor so derivative as Hood, and he is not given to Augustan moralizing. Hood's lines 47–69, for example, remind us less of Keats than of Thomas Gray, another favorite of Hood's. Our final judgment on "Ode to Melancholy" must be that it reveals the poet's penchant for the morbid mainly in the style and language of other poets. It is less independent and "authentic" than Hood's better creations in its genre and hence less interesting.

Hood's greatest achievement in the realm of terror before 1829 was "Lycus, the Centaur," one of the three major pieces in *Midsummer Fairies.* Hood, perhaps anticipating the reader's difficulty in following this tale of 114 tetrameter couplets,[18] epitomized it in a preceding "Argument": "Lycus, detained by Circe in her magical dominion, is beloved by a Water Nymph, who desiring to render him immortal, has recourse to the Sorceress. Circe gives her an incantation to pronounce, which should turn Lycus into a horse; but the horrible effect of the charm causing her to break off in the midst, he becomes a Centaur." [19] Circe's revenge is even more cruel than she had dreamed, for Lycus is now a monster hated by man and beast alike. Finally, he wanders to Thessaly, where he is left to an uncertain fate among others of his kind.

The real distinction of "Lycus" is emphatically as a tale of terror and not as a revival of myth. Viewed in the latter aspect, the story has little originality,[20] being essentially a retelling of the account of Glaucus, Scylla, and Circe in Book III of Keats's *Endymion*—[21] an old tale which Hood very likely knew also from Ovid's *Metamorphoses* (XIII) and Lempriere's *Classical Dictionary.* Catullus' "Attis" (*Carmina,* LXIII) could also have been a partial source. Aside from a slight parallel in the stories of Lycus and Attis, both of whom suffer a tragic change through a goddess's jealousy, there is a broad resemblance in tempo: the anapestic tetrameters of Hood are a far cry from Catullian galliambics, but both meters manage to convey a rushing, feverish urgency.

This urgency is intensified in "Lycus" by the use of the first person; the poem, in fact, has the quality of a long dramatic soliloquy. The opening couplet, somewhat Dantesque—[22] "Who hath ever been lured and bound by a spell / To wander, foredoom'd, in that circle of hell"—hurries us into the long introductory question and through it to the initial personal note in line nine. The tone of terror is firmly set in lines 13–28, especially when Lycus says

> And I gave me to slumber, as if from one dream
> To another—each horrid—and drank of the stream
> Like a first taste of blood, lest as water I quaff'd
> Swift poison, and never should breathe from the draught—
> Such drink as her own monarch husband drain'd up
> When he pledg'd her, and Fate clos'd his eyes in the cup.
> And I pluck'd of the fruit with held breath, and a fear
> That the branch would start back and scream out in my ear;
> For once, at my suppering, I pluck'd in the dusk
> An apple, juice-gushing and fragrant of musk;
> But by daylight my fingers were crimson'd with gore,
> And the half-eaten fragment was flesh at the core;
>
> (ll. 17–28)

There is a special blend of horror and pathos in the description of Circe's victims, animals that were once men, that "hung down their heads with a human-like shame" (ll. 64–71). The contemporaries of Hood who knew him only as the poet of *Odes and Addresses* must have been stunned by his catalogue of awful creatures that emerge from the gloom like a hideous tangle of spiders and scorpions from a dank cellar (ll. 130–35). Hood's blending of mythical monsters with gruesomely realistic details—"sharp beaks and wide gaping of jaws, / With flapping of wings, and fierce grasping of claws, / And whirls of long tails" (ll. 140–42) —thickens our marrow almost as much as do comparable passages in Spenser, Milton, or Dante. Another scene worth particular attention is the one picturing the coruscating, almost psychodelic metamorphoses of Circe (11. 300 ff.). But perhaps the most moving episode in the story, because of its sensitive and dramatic depiction of the terror of utter loneliness, is that in which the abhorred Centaur finds love in his encounter with a kindly boy— only to have the relationship tragically destroyed through a misunderstanding (11. 384–409). (While resisting the temptation to read too much symbolism into the poem, might we cautiously theorize that this is Hood's sad commentary on human relationships?)

"Lycus, the Centaur" is brought to a close soon after the incident just sketched, with Lycus in wild Thessaly among the other Centaurs; we are not told whether he found fellowship with them and became reconciled to his lot. Although it is difficult to quarrel with Hood's decision to leave the eventual fate of his hero clouded in mystery, even his kindest critic must admit that the closing lines are muddled and awkward:

> . . . I have heard how they met by a stream
> In games, and were suddenly changed by a scream
> That made wretches of many, as she roll'd her wild eyes
> Against heav'n, and so vanish'd.—The gentle and wise
> Lose their thoughts in deep studies, and others their ill
> In the mirth of mankind where they mingle them still.

Today's critics of "Lycus" do not agree about its merit, nor did they in Hood's day; [23] but all have conceded it to be an extraordinary work. It was, as Rossetti says,[24] Hood's annunciation of himself as a new poet to be reckoned with. Inevitably, some have found psychological autobiography in the poem. Heath-Stubbs, for example, sees the story as a kind of autotherapy, an imaginative construct of the world as it appeared to a poet oppressed by illness, frustration, and anxiety.[25] The theory is reasonable, but we wish that Heath-Stubbs would explain whether or not he considers this a *conscious* purpose on Hood's part. It will be necessary to glance at this line of interpretation again in connection with "The Haunted House." Heath-Stubbs's deeper interpretation of the poem, particularly of the encounter between Lycus and the boy, as symbolic myth must be reluctantly rejected on the ground that it exaggerates Hood's mythopoeic faculty.[26] We must not underestimate Hood, but neither should we see him as another Shelley or Blake. When all is said, most readers are likely to feel with Saintsbury that, although "Lycus, the Centaur" "has some false notes," it "is admirable as a whole." [27]

IV "The Dream of Eugene Aram"

Thomas Hood's most remarkable probing into the dark arcana of the lonely human soul is found in "The Dream of Eugene Aram, the Murderer" (1829).[28] The actual history of Eugene Aram (1704–59) is itself strange and fascinating,[29] for he was a most uncommon criminal. By profession an usher (that is, a tutor) at the Lynn School for boys in Norfolk, Aram was a keen student of languages. Although self-taught as a linguist, he was the first scholar to identify the Celtic tongues as belonging to the Indo-European family of languages. In 1758, Aram was suddenly arrested for the murder of a former friend, committed fourteen years earlier, and was subsequently hanged at Newgate Prison. To all appearances, this man was a dedicated (if eccentric) scholar; moreover, a distinguished alumnus of Lynn reported that Aram was "beloved of the boys" there.[30] Hardly the typical felon who swung from Newgate scaffold! There is a Dostoevskian quality in the story of this murderer. It brings a terrible focus on the complex and chameleon nature of good and evil—possibly the one abstract idea that is irresistible to any mind capable of abstraction. It was particularly so to Hood, whose interest in the peculiar and pathological went far beyond the common measure.

The stanzaic form of "Eugene Aram" is familiar to us through "The Sea-Spell" and "The Last Man": it is the six-line unit used here and there in Coleridge's "The Ancient Mariner." Hood's poem has other things in common with Coleridge's: both are studies in guilt and remorse, and there are some verbal parallels which, though not strikingly close, are suggestive: "lifeless flesh and bone" (Hood, 11. 90–91) and "lifeless lump" (Coleridge, 1. 218); "There was a manhood in his look, / That murder could not kill" (Hood, 11. 95–96) and "the curse in a dead man's eye" (Coleridge, 1. 260); "And, lo! the universal air / Seem'd lit with ghastly flame" (Hood, 11. 97–98) and "The upper air burst into life! / And a hundred fire-flags sheen" (Coleridge, 11. 313–15); "All night I lay in agony" (Hood, 11. 145, 151) and "My soul in agony" (Coleridge, 1. 235). It is doubtful, however, that we should note these comparisons were it not for Hood's known admiration for Coleridge; for "Eugene Aram" is distinctively "Hood's own."

An analysis of Hood's techniques in this poem discovers no new ones, but the familiar ones are used with a competence that makes "Eugene Aram" still one of the best things of its kind. The opening lines sketch a deceptively charming semi-pastoral setting. (By 1829 Hood was an old hand at exploiting paradoxes.) The schoolboys come bounding out of the classroom in innocent high spirits—then their mirth and guiltlessness are thrown against the melancholy and remorse of the usher, Aram (11. 18–36). Yet the suddenness is not awkward, for the remark that the boys' souls are "untouched by sin" inclines us to suspect that a contrast will follow, somewhat in the manner of Gray's "Ode on a Distant Prospect of Eton College." Indeed, it is not idle to compare the two poems; for Gray, after describing the innocent joy of the sportive Etonians, laments that they will be overtaken by "black Misfortune's baleful train" and racked by "the fury Passions" (11. 55–70). Aram, once as pure and artless as the lad he addresses, has suffered this fate. We have seen that Hood once parodied Gray's famous work,[31] and we need not be overimaginative to glimpse some grisly shadows of it in "The Dream of Eugene Aram."

Hood proceeds to dramatize the aforementioned contrast, through a kind of Blakean confrontation of Innocence and Experience, when he has Aram approach a young boy sitting in the shade with his eyes fixed on a book—which, almost too aptly, proves to be *The Death of Abel*—but only "almost," for several reasons. In the first place, the Swiss author Salomon Gessner's work of this title was very popular in England.[32] A special irony is achieved by having the guileless boy engrossed in a story of murder; and only a critic singularly unobservant of children's behavior would see anything abnormal in this situation. The pertinency of a story of murder to the poem as a whole needs no demonstration; the point is that the subject of the lad's book lends credibility to Aram's long discourse on manslaughter which follows. We are told that the historical Aram did in fact make such speeches to his pupils; [33] we presume that a man of Aram's intelligence—a respected teacher with no desire to look suspiciously eccentric—would always find an appropriate point of departure for these lectures, doubtless presenting as moral instruction what was in fact an agonizing autopsychotherapy.

The Aram of the poem, like Raskolnikov in Dostoevsky's *Crime and Punishment,* seems under compulsion to confess his crime, and yet he dares not. By relating his murder as a dream, using the first person, Aram can disburden himself (to a degree at least) without danger of the scaffold—or so he thinks. The fact is that the police are already on their way to apprehend him. But Aram does not know this development, and neither do we until the very last stanza, where Hood deftly combines the stylistic qualities of abruptness and restraint with the emotional ones of pathos and horror:

> That very night, while gentle sleep
> The urchin eyelids kiss'd,
> Two stern-faced men set out from Lynn,
> Through the cold and heavy mist;
> And Eugene Aram walked between,
> With gyves upon his wrist.

Hood provides no opportunity for the inner orgy of half-sadistic emotion that a detailed account of the execution might arouse, nor does he constrain the reader's imagination within the strait-jacket of conventional moralizing. His laconic starkness evokes pure pity and horror by forcing a direct confrontation with tragedy. Here Thomas Hood, the Romantic, touches hands with the masters of Realism.

It remains to say a few words on the language of "Eugene Aram." Its intensity shows how deeply the poet entered imaginatively into the mind of a man who, no criminal by inclination, had yet committed a terrible crime. This quality is heightened by the simplicity of Hood's vocabulary, as in these lines:

> All night I lay in agony,
> In anguish dark and deep;
> My fever'd eyes I dared not close,
> But stared aghast at Sleep:
> For Sin had render'd unto her
> The keys of Hell to keep!
> (11. 145–50)

The comparatively few abstractions and personifications in "Eugene Aram" are, like those in the preceding passage, natural and unforced even in the most rhetorical parts of the poem (11. 133–44); for a man so steeped in learning as Aram would unconsciously fall into biblical, Shakespearean, and Miltonic patterns in his most impassioned utterances.

The combination of intensity and simplicity, a kind of "essentiality," in the language of "Eugene Aram" hits especially hard in the usher's self-torturing emphasis upon the appalling brutality of his crime:

> Two sudden blows with a ragged stick,
>   And one with a heavy stone,
> One hurried gash with a hasty knife,—
>   And then the deed was done:
> There was nothing lying at my foot
>   But lifeless flesh and bone!
>   (11. 85–90)

The transferred epithet "hasty knife" conveys powerfully both the savagery and the desperate urgency of the deed. And few of us can repress a shudder as the murderer cries out in mortal terror,

> Ay, though he's buried in a cave,
>   And trodden down with stones,
> And years have rotted off his flesh,—
>   The world shall see his bones!
>   (11. 195–98)

Finally, as in certain other poems, Hood sometimes distributes an alliterative effect throughout several lines or even a complete stanza, as in "agony," "anguish," "aghast" (11. 145–50). Among examples from portions of the work not quoted above are "blessed breeze," "burning . . . brow," "bosom," "book between" (11. 20–24) and "fast and fervent," "fixed"; "close," "could . . . close," "clasp . . . clasp" (11. 32–36).

Even after this rather lengthy analysis, it must be stressed that only a full reading of "The Dream of Eugene Aram" can yield its total sustained effect.

V *"The Elm-Tree"* and Shorter Pieces

Many years after his creation of "Eugene Aram," Hood attempted a more pretentious work in the realm of terror with "The Elm-Tree: A Dream in the Woods," which he contributed to the *New Monthly Magazine* in September, 1842. Formally, this longish (492 lines) quasi-mythic poem is divided into three parts and is written mainly in the Coleridgean stanza of "Eugene Aram"; in seventeen of the seventy-nine stanzas, a dimeter couplet is used in lines 1–2, 3–4, or 5–6.

"The Elm-Tree" tells of a mysterious forest dominated by a stately elm and of a marauding woodcutter who lays waste the region. After he has left the scene, a "grisly Phantom" appears and discourses for eighty-two lines on the theme that the great fallen tree, now the victim of proud, selfish man, will hold man's remains in the end. The macabre note is personalized somewhat as the poet senses

A secret, vague, prophetic gloom,
    As though by certain mark
I knew the fore-appointed Tree,
    Within whose rugged bark
This warm and living frame shall find
    Its narrow house and dark.
                                        (ll. 481–86)

Knowing Hood as a man whose continual battle with illness might well have led him to expect an early death, we do not find it incongruous that an author famed in his time as a "funny man" should have written such lines. On this ground, the poem claims our sympathies.

Regrettably, however, our over-all response to "The Elm-Tree" as a work of art is one of disappointment. Hood seems not to have made up his mind what kind of piece he meant to write; and, as often happens in poetry, the result of this unsureness and lack of focus is a work that is fussily elaborate and rhetorical. The story vaguely suggests the Greek myth of Erysichthon, who was cursed with insatiable hunger after ravaging a tree inhabited by a hamadryad in a sacred Thessalian grove. Although Erysichthon is not mentioned in the poem, lines 40–45, beginning "O hath the Dryad still a tongue," suggest that Hood did have the myth in mind.

On the other hand, Hood seems to be recounting a highly personal experience, a dream that he might actually have had. Had he confined himself to this aim, "The Elm-Tree" would probably be a good poem; it might be an even better one had Hood effected an organic fusion of the mythic and the personal instead of just throwing them into one basket. Occasionally, Hood approaches his best efforts in the evocation of terror, as in some of the lines describing the "sad and solemn sound" emanating from the mysterious tree (for example, lines 8–13, 89–94).

But the total effect is marred by what can only be called prolixity and affectedness. (This fault, seen in the earlier "Ode to Melancholy," was never fully overcome by Hood.) Too many stanzas are required to tell about the sounds of the enchanted tree and the appearance of the woodcutter. The impression is inescapable that a plethora of conceits and descriptive phrases came easily—too easily—to Hood as he wrote the poem and that he was unable to part with any of them. "The Elm-Tree" is shot through with locutions that might be acceptable in a work akin to Keats's *Endymion* or to Coleridge's "Christabel," but the profusion of words like "e'en," "e'er," "mayhap," "perchance," and "recks" jars against the personal and contemporary impression left by some parts of the poem. There are too many phrases like "fleecy clouds," "leafy roof," and "yonder dell" that had overserved their duty well before 1800. The monotony of the twenty-eight phrases beginning with "No," used mostly to stress the absence of life in the haunted forest ("No breeze," "No bird," etc.), is a very different thing from the inspired use of repetition that we shall see in "The Haunted House."

A curious feature of "The Elm-Tree" is the richness of its natural history: eighteen kinds of animal and twenty-three types of plant life are mentioned, excluding wholly figurative allusions. Now and then Hood's descriptions of wildlife show sensitive observation and a genuine feeling for the shy, secret life of forest creatures:

> A Cony from the sandy bank
>   Has run a rapid race,
> Through thistle, bent, and tangled fern,
>   To seek the open space;

And on its haunches sits erect
To clean its furry face.

(11. 338–43)

At other times, though, it must be admitted that Hood's pictures of animal life in "The Elm-Tree" are spoiled by awkwardness or triteness.[34]

Every artist has a right to his failures, and "The Elm-Tree" must be regarded as one of Hood's. Yet the poem is not a total disaster; for, as we have indicated, some lines are chillingly evocative and some show an authentic feeling for nature. If Hood had edited the piece more severely, if he had tried harder to give it unity of focus and treatment, the poem might compare favorably with "Eugene Aram" or with "The Haunted House." The probable truth is that he simply did not feel the subject strongly enough to make this effort.

Before climaxing this study of Hood's darker muse with "The Haunted House," we should briefly look at a few short poems, quite personal in subject and feeling, that show a preoccupation with death.[35] Two of these, "The Death-Bed" and "Anticipation," were probably written not long after the death of the poet's sister in 1831. (Both poems were published in the *Englishman's Magazine* in that year; the first in August, the second in September.) We should acknowledge at once that for a poet to disburden himself of personal grief through his poetry shows no special penchant for the morbid; nevertheless, an expression of this kind clearly has particular relevance to the case of Hood.

"The Death-bed," a little poem of sixteen lines in the familiar ballad quatrain, is remarkable chiefly for its use of chiasmus in the third stanza:

Our very hopes belied our fears
Our fears our hopes belied—
We thought her dying when she slept,
And sleeping when she died!

Here the poet just escapes a rhetorical expertise that might suggest an unbecoming "professionalism" toward his subject. (Indeed, it is extraordinary how often Hood skirts the boundary between excellence and impropriety.) He does escape it for most readers, however, because of the unmistakable tenderness that shines through the rhetoric. The poem's brevity, simplicity, and restraint show the containment of a feeling that is strong enough to need containing. These qualities are well illustrated by the final stanza:

> For when the morn came dim and sad—
> And chill with early showers,
> Her quiet eyelids closed—she had
> Another morn than ours!

"Anticipation" opens with the line "I had a vision in the summer light." In this clairvoyant moment, says the poet, he saw himself in the company of a beloved person (his sister?) on a gorgeous April morning. Suddenly "an invisible fear / Shook in the trees and chill'd upon the air" (11. 22-23); and a terrible shadow fell, "Like a dark pall," over the form of this cherished woman. If the poem recounts an actual foreshadowing that Hood had of his sister's death before she became seriously ill (rather than a backward transference of sorrow intensified by contrast with a previous joy), it might be cited as evidence of a genuine morbidity in Hood. The evidence would be stronger could it be shown that the subject of the poem is not Hood's sister but some imaginary beloved or even an image of the poet's own life. Such matters can never be settled, especially when, as in this case, the precise relationship between the date of *composition* of the poem and that of the event it deals with can never be established.

"Stanzas: Is there a bitter pang" is a thorny poem to handle because it seems so personal and yet is so elusive of any effort to relate it specifically to the author's life. (The poem is of uncertain date and was published posthumously, but it is surely a late work.) Here is the last of its three regular stanzas:

> Would I had never filled thine eyes with love,
>   For love is only tears: would I had never
> Breathed such a curse-like blessing as we prove:
>   Now, if 'Farewell' could bless thee, I would sever!
>   Would I were laid
>   Under the shade
> Of the cold tomb, and the long grass for ever!

The death wish is felt throughout the poem. If it is autobiographical, as seems undeniable, we are at a loss to identify the addressee unless it be the poet's wife—a solution that seems unsatisfactory because of Thomas and Jane's known compatibility and mutual devotedness. Still, Hood could have written these lines in an agony of remorse over the trouble and anxiety suffered by his wife *because* of her attachment to him. (Those who believe that the poem was addressed to Mrs. Hood [though surely not for her eyes] might find it interesting to compare "Stanzas" with Byron's "Fare Thee Well.") Possibly this work is an instance of Hood's turning to poetry as a partial release from inner pain—a kind of self-therapy.

VI *"The Haunted House"*

Hood's macabre masterpiece, "The Haunted House," recalls Sir Walter Scott's comment on Horace Walpole's *The Castle of Otranto:* it makes an irresistible "appeal to that secret and reserved feeling of love for the marvellous and supernatural, which occupies a hidden corner in almost everyone's bosom." [36] The correctness of Scott's view is attested by the perennial popularity of "horror thrillers" in all media.

"The Haunted House" appeared in *Hood's Monthly Magazine* in January, 1844, about sixteen months before the writer's death. Technically, the work shows great care and competence, especially in view of its 352 lines—a somewhat risky length for a poem of terror that is primarily a mood piece rather than a narrative. A mark of Hood's skill is his use of a trimeter line to end each quatrain (except as noted below), the first three lines being five-stressed. This device prevents a monotonous regularity that would be fatal to the poet's purpose; the short line introduces a hint of uneasiness that abets this purpose: it is as if we were stopped short by some faint but eerie sound. Equally effective is the well-timed repetition of the following stanza, which occurs, with occasional variation in the first line, nine times in the poem:

> O'er all there hung a shadow and a fear;
> A sense of mystery the spirit daunted,
> And said, as plain as whisper in the ear,
> The place is Haunted!

This stanza is almost the one of Keats's "La Belle Dame sans Merci," the only difference being that Hood ends the second and fourth lines with an amphibrach rather than an iamb (or, for those preferring another nomenclature, with an iamb followed by an unaccented syllable). The short line with the amphibrach repeats *a fortiori* the effect of the short line in the basic stanza. Crispness and clarity, qualities so estimable in many works, are of all things to be shunned in a poem designed to produce sensations of undefinable malaise and fear. This stylized stanza is no mere refrain, for Hood achieves through its use an incremental dramatic quality that he climaxes by ending the poem with this stanza at the high point of terror. The poet is so paralyzed by his experience, we feel, that he can speak at all only by falling back upon ceremonial or formulaic utterance.

"The Haunted House" has little story as such. The narrator, in a dream, finds himself before "An old deserted Mansion," which he is strangely compelled to enter in spite of his fears. The courtyard is rubble-ridden and overgrown with vines and weeds; the somewhat "Gothic" interior presents a sad and unsettling scene of wasted and desolate grandeur. Secretive wild creatures, some of them sinister, have the run of the place. The trespasser moves through the house in a kind of trance until his gaze is transfixed by a banner bearing a sanguine hand that blazons out "ominously vivid" amidst the dilapidated flags, armor, and other feudal trappings. The same menacing design is projected on the stone floor through the only unbroken pane in the casement window. Finally, the dreamer enters a bedroom, where his blood suddenly drops to zero. There on the bed curtain is the bloody hand [37]—on the floor, leading from the bed to the window, is an irregular track of dark stains still recognizable as blood. "A ghostly Shadow" seems to flit across the room.

Many descriptive details would be called, in the general sense, Gothic: "iron gates," "weedy moat," "Ghostly hall," "heraldic banners," "taper burning bluely," "rich hangings," etc. There are also some animals, birds, and other creatures with Gothic associations: the eft, the spider, the centipede, the bat, the screech-owl, the "Death's Head moth," and the "Death Watch" (a clicking wood-beetle). Relics of the "Graveyard School" of poetry, sometimes indistinguishable from those of Gothicism, crowd one another in the poem: in, for example, the first four stanzas of Part II. "The Haunted House" thus contains some conventional images and phraseology, but they lend themselves perfectly to the mood of the piece and do not seem either trite or obtrusive.

The gradation of tempo and intensity within the poem demands special notice. It opens on an almost conversational note, with the poet musing in a rather detached way about the nature of dreams and of the imaginative process. His account of the dream content itself is at first played pianissimo, as the persona of the story approaches the old mansion, passes the gate, and walks through the courtyard—slowly, it would seem, since he describes in some detail the ruin that he sees and the antics of the usurping wildlife. (Actually, he does not push the door open until line 145.) We are not allowed to forget that "The place is Haunted!" (11. 32, 116); but, in Part I, Hood's emphasis is mainly upon the desolation and eerie loneliness of the ancient house. The only real hint of the horror to come is in the lines "Some weighty crime, that Heaven could not pardon, / A secret curse on that old building hung" (11. 66–67)—and, at this stage in the poem, such words could express no more than an inference that might be made by anyone familiar with tales of haunted houses and ancestral curses. Hood shows a most judicious restraint in holding back the direr portents for Part II. The story mounts steadily in dread intensity as the dreamer pushes open the ancient door, walks fearfully through the hall, gazes, trembling, at the banner with its bloody hand, and (in Part III) makes his way up the "gloomy stairs" and into the fatal bedchamber.

Although "The Haunted House" has its share of Gothic décor, in one important respect it belongs in the "modern" tradition of such tales of terror as Henry James's *The Turn of the Screw,* Walter de la Mare's "All Hallows," and Algernon Blackwood's "The Willows." In dealing with the so-called supernatural, these authors rarely introduce anything that could not somehow be explained, as we say, "rationally." Yet, luckily for art, *nothing is really explained.* So it is in Hood's story of a haunting: there are no genuine, unmistakable "spooks"; and nothing happens that could not have a natural cause. The "Inexplicable tremors" that "shook the arras" (1. 310) could be caused by drafts or by the settling of the house; the ensanguined banner that "shone out / So ominously vivid" (11. 191–92) might be made of better stuff and stained with a faster dye than the graying rags around it; the "ghostly Shadow" (1. 344) could be created by the wind blowing a curtain or a bough outside the window. In short, there is no proof that infernal spirits are at work.

There *is* some evidence that a fearful crime was committed in the bedroom; and we can theorize from an earlier passage, that seems to point with shuddering evasiveness toward the tragedy, that this crime was a uxoricide or a mariticide:

> O very, very dreary is the room
> Where Love, domestic Love, no longer nestles,
> But smitten by the common stroke of doom,
> The Corpse lies on the trestles!
>
> (11. 121–24)

At the end of the dream, the figurative corpse—the death of love between husband and wife—is to be reified in the most terrible way. Lines 157–54 foreshadow more directly, especially through the phrases "dying victim" and "tale of murther." "The place is Haunted!"—but by an actual presence from the world behind the veil or by the survival, with all their evocativeness, of the physical stage and properties that witnessed the event? Hood wisely leaves the answer to the individual reader, for each has his own apperceptive mass and his own set of receptors.

Heretofore, we have focused on the elements of mystery and terror in "The Haunted House"; now its realistic aspects must have their due. For a work concerned less with the openly natural than with the putative supernatural, the mere variety of its wildlife is extraordinary: besides the creatures mentioned earlier, we find among the animals the rabbit, the rat, the frog, the lizard, and the toad; among the birds, the pigeon, the wren, the crow, the coot, the water-hen, the heron, the "Whitwall" (or witwall, a spotted woodpecker), and the jay; and, among the insects, the earwig, the ant ("emmet"), and wood-louse. The plants, especially the wild ones, have grown with fantastic vigor in man's absence. Turning briefly again to the animal world, we find a significant contrast between the innocent, carefree life of the woodland creatures and the turbulence and tragedy of human life: the wren builds her nest in the porch; the rabbit frisks "leisurely and bold"; the woodpecker and jay make the woods echo with their clamor.[38] But, for the human visitant, the atmosphere is one of fear and gloom; for all this tremendous vitality can only heighten his awareness of the deadness and decadence of all that is man-made about the place.

In the preceding paragraph, we see Hood as very much the *Romantic* poet, both in the specificity of his descriptions of wild nature and in his tendency to draw analogies, especially contrasting ones, between man and his humbler kin. In this respect, Hood is one of a numerous company that includes Burns, Wordsworth, Shelley, Keats, Bryant, and Thoreau. Furthermore, Hood shows the Romantic predilection for wild profusion—"The raggedness of nature" (1. 100)—over a nature controlled by man's passion for "order." In "The Haunted House" the free expression of these Romantic traits perfectly serves Hood's central purpose while maintaining a viability of its own.

It is conceivable that in "The Haunted House" Hood treats imaginatively an incident actually experienced in his waking hours; indeed, many people can recall a similar adventure. He teases us into thought with the words "in the spirit, *or in the flesh*" (1. 7)—[39] although presumably this ambiguity is intended to suggest that the memory of the dream is so vivid as to be indistinguishable from reality. But, regardless of what relationship, if any, the content of the poem has to Hood's outward experience, the fact remains that he *chose* to present it as a dream. Perhaps he did so to surmount the defenses of the skeptical reader since anything may be allowed in a dream; perhaps to remove the experience farther from the ordinary laws of time and space and thus make it more eerie. If we knew that Hood used the dream device simply out of fear that a "straight" approach might alienate the reader, then we would say that he should have been more confident of his powers.

One thing is sure: because the poet did use this device, thus placing the story in the realm of the private subconscious, many readers will be tempted to adopt in this case the psychoanalytic approach to interpretation that is so fascinating, so fashionable, and often (alas!) so facile and misleading. Just as we might see in Byron's "Darkness" a frightful picture of his inner ruin or in Poe's "The Haunted Palace" the account of a mind (perhaps the poet's own) driven toward madness, so the decaying, specter-ridden mansion described by Hood might be an iconographic revelation of a life haunted by illness, anxiety, and crumbled hopes.[40] It is certainly suggestive that Hood, like Byron,[41] implies that there is some truth in his poem:

> Some dreams we have are nothing else but dreams,
> Unnatural, and full of contradictions;
> Yet others of our most romantic schemes
> Are something more than fictions.

(ll. 1–4)

This statement could easily be interpreted to mean that the horrific content of "The Haunted House" has some special relevance to Hood's inner world. To examine closely a theory so speculative, so complex in its implications, and so impatient of proof would require many additional pages. For our purposes, it is enough to acknowledge that this poem is a masterpiece in the genre of the macabre and the grotesque.

CHAPTER 5

Hood as a Prose Writer

I Shorter Works: Sketches, Essays, Reviews

BEYOND question, Hood's chief fame rests on his poetry, and his stature as a poet is likely to increase as more and more "discoveries" are made about the minor Romantics. Hood's output of prose was, nevertheless, so enormous that it cannot be ignored in a study of this kind. It is simply impossible to cover the works in detail—a fact that should not be deeply mourned; for, with the exception of his separate books and a few of the shorter pieces, Hood's prose writings were never intended to be other than ephemeral. Practically all these works appeared first in periodicals, especially the *New Monthly Magazine,* the *Athenaeum,* and *Hood's Monthly Magazine;* many made a second appearance in the *Comic Annuals, Hood's Own,* and *Whimsicalities.*[1] The purpose of this survey is chiefly to give an impression of the range of subject matter and treatment found in Hood's prose. Since our concern is only with the works that he designed for publication, the letters—interesting though they are—are omitted.

Hood's first published work in prose, "A Sentimental Journey from Islington to Waterloo Bridge, in March, 1821,"[2] was one of his early contributions to the *London Magazine.* This sketch announces many of the hallmarks of Hood's later prose, especially that of a serio-whimsical, or Sternean, cast. The resemblances to Sterne are due in part to direct influence but also to a certain temperamental kinship between the two authors. The title of Hood's "Journey" is of course borrowed from Sterne's *A Sentimental Journey through France and Italy* (1768), and the sketch contains some specific references to Sterne.[3] More truly revealing of Sterne's influence are the loose, digressive, rambling structure, based on the free association of ideas; sentimentality, which often smiles at itself; abundant use of conversation, not all of it relevant, with numerous questions and interruptions; much philosophizing and moralizing, often with tongue halfway in cheek; and a mildly distracted view of practically everything.

The Sternean flavor of Hood's "Journey" is strongly sensed in both the nature of the adventures encountered by the hero and in Hood's treatment of them. For example, the sentimental journeyer arbitrates a quarrel between a husband and wife and then makes a long, ceremonial address on the sharing of sovereignty between the sexes. His peroration draws cheers and proffered drinks from men and women alike.[4] Hardly given time to enjoy his triumph, the hero is alarmed by the "shrill cry of a female in distress" and rushes to her aid. She turns out to be a young sow being thrashed by a brutal hog-drover, but the youth's chivalrous impulses are not therefore dampened. He has a short altercation with the drover, but, reluctant to "disfigure 'the human face divine'"—since "one of us, at least, was handsome"—he gives the ignorant ruffian a crown, urges coaxing instead of cruelty, and makes a brief speech to the bystanders on the art of "pig-driving." [5] As he continues his stroll through the crowded streets, the traveler speculates on the revelation of character through facial expression—confessing, however, his fallibility when it develops that the man with shifty eyes (obviously "afraid of bailiffs") is only looking for his stray poodle.[6] But the stroller's inveterate habit of philosophizing quickly reasserts itself as he analyzes his passion for window shopping in the Strand; and, browsing in the bookshops, he ponders the question whether "cultivation of the mind conduces to happiness." [7] In this part of the sketch the subtle but distinctive touch of Lamb is perhaps more discernible than that of Sterne.

Like most of the works reviewed in this chapter, Hood's "A Sentimental Journey" lacks real weight but is on the whole very entertaining. Stylistically, it is a remarkable performance for a man of twenty-two with a limited education; on the other hand, we must remember that Hood's basic prose style was formulated early and developed but little. His matter and treatment, however, show an impressive variety; and Hood certainly grew in maturity and in depth of insight. This growth is ably witnessed by "Literary Reminiscences" (1839), which superficially has much in common with "A Sentimental Journey": sentimental recollection; mischievous wit, fun, and irony, occasionally skirting the fantastic; light treatment of the serious and vice versa. "Literary Reminiscences" is a far more serious work, however, and is radically different in purpose, being essentially autobiographical. The portions of this work quoted in Chapter 2 [8] are sufficient to show its character, save for the fact that excerpts can only faintly convey the meandering structure of the work. Some might think this a fault, but free-associative digressiveness is always allowable in reminiscential writing so long as interest is sustained. Hood's ineptitude for sustained, unified narrative does him no harm in "Literary Reminiscences," and indeed many readers find this his most appealing and estimable prose work.[9] If it does not overwhelm us (never Hood's way), it seduces us with its free-ranging wit and whimsy, its graphic eyewitness description of famous literary figures, the author's obvious zest for his task, and —not least—the likable personality of Hood himself as it comes through in this very personal work.

The remainder of Hood's periodical prose can best be viewed through a selective survey that violates neither spatial limitations nor our spirit of courtesy toward the subject. Among the prose offerings of Hood that are on the light side and yet of some lasting value, "Johnsoniana" (1833) is enjoyed by every student of English literature. Purportedly a letter to the editor of the *Comic Annual* from "Septimus Reardon," the scholar-writer maintains that, despite the impression left by Dr. Samuel Johnson's aphorism that "he who would make a pun would pick a pocket," "the inimitable author of Rasselas did not dogmatically predicate such an aggravated degree of moral turpitude in the perpetration of a double entendre." [10] This sesquipedalian thesis is supported by an alleged list of very entertaining puns from Dr. Johnson's conversations. Our awareness that Hood himself was the most inveterate punster who ever lived helps to season this agreeable side dish.

Hood's capacity for amusing nonsense is also seen in two essays on the same subject, "Queries in Natural History" and "Speculations of a Naturalist" (both 1839). He first considers such scientific questions as whether flies can read. To prove the affirmative, the example is cited of a Dublin merchant who changed the sign on his shop from "Grocer" to "Tobacconist" because the former had attracted a bothersome horde of flies.[11] Of the several puns in this treatise, the best—and most outrageous—is at the end, where a physician prescribes a "kittenplasm" instead of a cataplasm because the patient is a child.[12] "Speculations of a Natural-ist" discusses the mentality of the oyster: "Does it ever get to its wits' end—or even to their beginning?" [13] Hood's love of the final pun appears in the observation that "an Oyster is very anoma-lous" because "you must take it out of its bed before you can tuck it in!" [14] Many of Hood's essays reflect this strain of pleasant "nuttiness."

Somewhat higher on the esthetic scale are two pieces that grew out of Hood's sojourn on the Continent: "The Schoolmistress Abroad: An Extravaganza" (1839) and "Fishing in Germany" (1840). "Fishing in Germany," much the slighter of these two works, is a casually dramatized conversation between "Amicus" (Hood) and "Lieutenant Von Piscator" (Lieutenant Phillip De Franck, Hood's good friend and fishing companion); but two other characters chime in occasionally. The work is agreeably diverting by virtue of its genial, low-gear humor; and, inciden-tally, it reveals Hood's rather detailed knowledge of the angler's art.

The provincial, straitlaced but likable English (or American) tourist on the Continent is a perennial subject for humor, and Hood does not fail it. The structure of "The Schoolmistress Abroad" is chaotic, with only the itinerary to give it form; yet, because of the fecklessness, confusion, and ill-luck of the trav-elers, there is a certain structural propriety here (though we suspect it to be accidental). Some good situational comedy arises from the challenges to the young governess' modesty caused by such things as ships' ladders and "the Mer Maladie." [15] Much is made of the wretched living conditions in Germany, which Hood himself complained about sometimes; perhaps we hear him speaking through Miss Crane's opinion that Swift must have de-rived his idea for the Houyhnhnms from the Germans who treat horses better than men.[16] On the other hand, we find in the next chapter a merciless caricature of the bigoted tourist who hates not only everything foreign but also "everybody who doesn't hate every thing foreign": who hates the Germans, the Dutch, the Americans, "all authors—except Dr. Johnson" (who, Mrs. Piozzi said, "was a very good hater"), and the aristocracy (because "they have such prejudices"!).[17]

Many comic tidbits in "The Schoolmistress Abroad" are pro-duced by Miss Crane's ignorance of modern foreign languages

and by her dependence upon her sister Ruth, the "linguist of
Lebanon house"—a classic case of the blind leading the blind. The
repeated query "Ruth, what is . . . ?" ("yar vole," "forstend nix,"
"gefallish," "krank") soon begins to elicit an automatic chuckle
from the reader. Ruth says of "krank," "In English, it's a thing
that helps to pull the bell." [18] However, "The Schoolmistress
Abroad" is not wholly lacking in serious thought. The concluding
paragraph, for example, parallels very briefly Hood's strictures
on the English educational system in "Literary Reminiscences": [19]
"For my own part," says Miss Crane, "I have met with a lesson
that has taught me my own unfitness for a Governess. For I cannot think that a style of education which has made me so helpless
and useless as a daughter, can be the proper one for young fe-
males, who are hereafter to become wives and mothers, a truth
that every hour has impressed on me since I have been a Schoolmistress Abroad." [20] It is surely significant that Hood chose to
end his "Extravaganza" on this particular note.

Another of Hood's more worthwhile prose entertainments with
some edificatory implications is "The Happiest Man in England"
(1839). Like many essays and sketches by Hood, this one evokes
the spirit of Lamb: it is unhurried, reflective, mildly satirical,
and engrossing without making great demands on the reader.
These qualities are seen in Hood's definition of the Optimist:

> The stranger . . . was an Optimist;—one of those blessed beings (for
> they are blessed) who think that whatever is is beautiful as well as
> right; practical philosophers, who make the best of everything; imag-
> inative painters, who draw each object *en beau,* and deal plentifully
> in *couleur de rose.* And they are right. To be good—in spite of all the
> old story-books, and all their old morals,—is not to be happy. The
> source of felicity, as the poet truly declares, is in the Mind—for like
> my fellow-traveller, the man who has a mind to be happy will be so,
> on the plainest commons that nature can set before him—with or
> without the rooks.[21]

The sketch approaches its humorous climax when the narrator
tells of an inspection visit that he makes to a plot of country land
advertised for sale (we are reminded of present-day promotion
schemes offering "resort" lots at unbelievably low prices). Who
should suddenly appear at the writer's elbow but the Optimist
himself, with a predictably rhapsodic comment on the landscape.
As he describes in lustrous terms this "demi-paradise," which is

actually a rural disaster area of weeds and mud, we are touched with envy of this man who sees only beauty in everything—until we learn "by chance" that he is a land auctioneer who makes a point of staying in practice! [22]

The genre known as the "character," familiar since Theophrastus, is revived briefly in Hood's impression of the Optimist; but it appears in a more classic and more savage form in "The Undertaker" (1839). The style is somewhat Lambian, but the tone is more reminiscent of Swift. One notable thing about this extended definition, besides its unfriendliness toward the subject, is its mixing of long and short sentences in such a way as to create a kind of rough impetuosity combined with rhetorical richness and urbanity:

> To be friends with an Undertaker is as impossible as to be the Crony of a Crocodile. He is by Trade a Hypocrite, and deals of Necessity in Mental Reservations and Equivoques. Thus he drinks to your good Health, but hopes, secretly, it will not endure. He is glad to find you so hearty—as to be Apoplectic. . . . He bids you beware of your old Gout—and recommends a Quack Doctor. He laments the malignant Fever so prevalent—and wishes you may get it. He compliments your Complexion—when it is Blue or Yellow; admires your upright Carriage,—and hopes it will break down. Wishes you good Day, but means everlasting Night. . . .
>
> To conclude, he is a Personage of ill presage to the House of Life: a Raven on the Chimney Pot—a Deathwatch in the Wainscot,—a Winding Sheet in the Candle.[23]

There is a temptation to relate Hood's bellicosity in this macabre piece to his valetudinarianism and thence to biographize and psychologize in the manner attempted briefly in Chapter 4. Hood, however, has not been the only author to stigmatize the hypocrisy and cupidity of some undertakers, as every reader of Dickens' *Great Expectations* or Evelyn Waugh's *The Loved One* is quite aware.

Moral indignation and social criticism on a more constructive plane distinguish "Copyright and Copywrong," a series of three letters published by Hood in the *Athenaeum* not long before he left Coblenz for Ostend in the summer of 1837. That Hood's interest in the rights of authors was not momentary is witnessed by two more *Athenaeum* letters about the same subject published in the summer of 1842. Hood was a militant and loyal supporter of Serjeant [24] Thomas Noon Talfourd's attempt to revise the existing laws so as to give authors a perpetual copyright on their works. The effort was, of course, a failure, although the status of authors was to be improved about five years later by the Copyright Act of 1842. Talfourd's work doubtless paved the way for this event, and possibly Hood's spirited and well-argued letters did their bit toward producing the climate of public thought that must always exist if reform legislation succeeds. In this respect, Hood again asserts his kinship with the earlier Romantics, who often served as Socratic gadflies.[25]

"Copyright and Copywrong" is a fairly long piece (the three letters written in 1837 cover thirty-six pages in the *Works*), and it is not easily represented through brief extracts. The following passage from the first letter, however, sounds the general temper and substance of the work: "We have neither character to lose nor property to protect. We are by law—outlaws, undeserving of civil rights. We may be robbed, libelled, outraged with impunity, being at the same time liable, for such offenses, to all the rigour of the code. I will not adduce, as I could do, a long catalogue of the victims of this system which seems to have been drawn up by the 'Lord of Misrule,' and sanctioned by the 'Abbot of Unreason.' " [26] Throughout, Hood never abandons his wit but uses it carefully and tellingly to project and support his serious arguments. These letters on copyright should be read in full by all who have any interest in the status of authors and in the law of property right as it applies to products of the mind.

More in Hood's familiar comic style, but like "Copyright and Copywrong" in that it expresses his indignation over man's inhumanity to man, is "The Black and White Question" (1839). Here Hood reveals his concern over the unjust treatment of Negroes, a feeling of which there are hints in some of his other works (for example, "The Doves and the Crows" and "A Black Job"). The argument is developed mainly through comparison: Hood contrasts the none too enviable situation of white apprentices in the colonies with the simply appalling one of so-called Negro apprentices, who in reality are little better than slaves— although slavery had been abolished throughout the British Empire about six years before the writing of this essay. Even "the Climbing Boy [chimney sweep], compared with the African, is almost a spoiled child." [27] "For my own part," Hood seriously concludes, "I cannot help thinking that the whole system of apprenticeship . . . requires to undergo a serious revision. . . ."[28] We cannot dodge the fact that there are things in "The Black and White Question" offensive to present-day members of the black race: they will not take kindly to Hood's calling his fictional informant "Sambo" or to his condescending attitude in general. Seen in historical perspective, however, Hood's efforts seem to ally him with those men of good will who are still searching for answers to "The Black and White Question."

Hood wrote a number of what would now be regarded as short stories (besides the *National Tales,* to be considered shortly). If he has a favorite genre here, it is what we might loosely style the Gothic: "The Apparition" (1839), "A Tale of the Great Plague" (1839), "The Grimsby Ghost" (1844), "A Tale of Terror" (1844).[29] Of these stories, only the last two are distinctive enough to warrant discussion in this survey. "The Grimsby Ghost," another work strongly suggesting the influence of Sterne, adopts a dilatory, whimsical approach: the actual story only gets under way in the second chapter. The narrative technique is the familiar one of having the adventure recounted by a superstitious, though obviously educated and "philosophical," storyteller to a matter-of-fact listener who breaks in now and then to ask questions and make random comments. The plot concerns a penny-pinching shopkeeper who, taken ill while entering a small sale in her ledger, tries desperately to impart a death-bed message. The secret, unfortunately, dies with her. Finally, though, after several ghostly appearances, Mrs. Mullins' spirit reveals the mystery—one so momentous and suspenseful that it must be honored with a separate chapter: *"Mary! it arn't booked—but there's tuppence for sandpaper at number nine!"* [30] That is all of the thirteenth and final chapter—and all of the story.

"A Tale of Terror," which Hood purposely left unfinished,[31] relates the nightmarish predicament of an "aëronaut" (balloonist) trapped hundreds of feet in the air with an assistant who turns out to be a dangerous maniac. Driven to superfrenzy by his fear of being returned to the madhouse, the lunatic insists on divesting the craft of all ballast (even to his own clothing) so that it will be carried out to sea. The aeronaut naturally resists and thereby infuriates his companion, who grabs the hero in a gorilla-like hug—and there the story ends!

As a busy magazine writer and editor Hood had many duties, one of which was to review numerous books. Of these reviews, the only ones apt to create much interest now are those of well-remembered works, a criterion which makes the present task of selection an easy one. The first issue of *Hood's Monthly Magazine* in January, 1840, contained a review by the editor of one of the best-known and most popular stories in the English language: Dickens' *A Christmas Carol,* published as a "Christmas book" in 1843. Hood's review, a large part of which is quotation, offers little genuine criticism, being primarily an "appreciation" that can still be read with pleasure by those who love Dickens' story. A brief sample indicates the general tone of the review:

> It was a blessed inspiration that put such a book into the head of Charles Dickens; a happy inspiration of the heart, that warms every page. It is impossible to read, without a glowing bosom and burning cheeks, between love and shame for our kind, with perhaps a little touch of misgiving, whether we are not personally open, a crack or so, to the reproach of Wordsworth,
> "The world is too much with us, early and late,
> Getting and spending."
> Whether our own heads have not become more inaccessible, our hearts more impregnable, our ears and eyes more dull and blind, to sounds and sights of human misery. . . . In a word, whether we have not grown *Scroogy?* [32]

A far more substantial specimen of the literary review is Hood's article on the first part of Dickens' *Master Humphrey's Clock* in the *Athenaeum* for November, 1840. Since this critique was much enjoyed by Dickens, it probably marked the beginning of the warm attachment that was formed between the two authors.[33] This remark might suggest the inference that Hood's review of *Master Humphrey's Clock* is simply an appreciation like the one of *A Christmas Carol* or that it is entirely laudatory, if not flattering. Actually, Hood begins on a rather severe note (for him), and approximately the first quarter of the piece is mainly unfavorable. Hood finds the narrative framework of the novel—specifically, the device of using Humphrey as narrator, in association with other loquacious characters outside the story—cumbersome and even superfluous. Dickens apparently came to feel the same way, for he abandoned this device after the first few chapters and changed the name of his book to *The Old Curiosity Shop.*

The remainder of the article, wholly favorable, reveals above all Hood's delight in the characterizations of Dickens. Though less restrained than most reviews are today, the piece is not merely whimsical or indiscriminate. For example, Hood's remark on the precocity of Little Nell shows considerable insight: "As for little Nelley herself, we should say that she thinks, speaks, and acts, in a style beyond her years, if we did not know how poverty and misfortune are apt to make advances of worldly knowledge to the young at a most ruinous discount—a painful sacrifice of the very capital of childhood. Like some of the patent sharpeners that give a hasty edge to the knife, at the expense of a rapid waste of metal, so does care act on the juvenile spirit."[34] Incidentally, this passage gives another glimpse of Hood's interest in social problems (a subject discussed in Chapter 6). The same can be said of Hood's words on Dick Swiveller: "There are thousands of Swivellers growing, or grown up, about town; neglected, ill-conditioned profligates, who owe their misconduct not to a bad bringing up, but to having no bringing up at all. Human hulks cast loose on the world. . . . Such an estray is Dick Swiveller. . . ."[35] Hood shows, for his day, a surprisingly "modern" view of delinquency. Finally, Hood's portrait of the fantastic Daniel Quilp is almost as unforgettably grotesque as the character himself: "Stunted in body and limbs, but with a head fit for a giant, and rough coarse hands, furnished with long, crooked, and yellow nails, he is described as a sort of human Caliban, who plots mischief and misery with the relentless malignity of a fiend, and fights, bites, and pinches with the wanton malice of a monkey."[36]

Unlike some critics who apply (without understanding it) the Horatian *nil admirari* and who quickly retreat into pseudo-sophisticated banality when betrayed by an unguarded disclosure of real enthusiasm, Hood is a Blakean critic for whom "enthusiastic admiration is the first principle of knowledge." This propensity enables him to put his finger on what is, for most readers, of permanent appeal in Dickens: "We invariably rise from the perusal of his volumes in better humour with the world, for he gives us a cheerful view of human nature, and paints good people with a relish which proves that he has himself a belief in, and sympathy with, their goodness. Moreover, he shows them to us . . . shining in clusters, as if he would fain have a milky way of

them; whereas he puts forward the bad as rarities or exceptions. . . ." [37]

As we remarked earlier, the dismaying bulk of Hood's prose
work precludes anything approaching a thorough survey. The
preceding selection from his shorter pieces should, however, give
us at least a feeling of familiarity with the main features of Hood's
work in this area. There remain to be considered his book-length
prose efforts: *National Tales, Tylney Hall, Up the Rhine,* and the
uncompleted *Our Family.*

II National Tales

We will recall that in 1826 Hood, with two successive publishing triumphs under his belt, was already feeling some dissatisfac-
tion over his image as a comic writer and was determined to
produce "some things of a more serious tone." [38] That the young
author's intent was "more serious" than the context of the statement itself was evidenced by his publication in February, 1827, of
National Tales, a collection of twenty-five stories concerning star-
crossed lovers, amiable or wicked schemers and tricksters, fantastic ventures, incredible sufferings, and so on—all familiar elements
to us, as to Hood's contemporaries, through the works of Boccaccio and Bandello and their imitators, the Gothic romances, and
the *Gesta Romanorum.* There are also possible echoes of Hellenic
romancers like Heliodorus and Longus [39] and of *Don Quixote;* [40]
some of the lighter stories [41] occasionally recall *A Hundred Merry
Tales* or other jest books of the Renaissance.

Among the features of the *National Tales* suggesting the possible influences just listed are the extravagant, melodramatic language, lachrymose sentimentality, Gothic horror and terror,
outrageous coincidence (both tragic and comic), and weighty
emphasis on poetic justice and moral edification. The tales are
about equally divided among the comic, the tragic, and the melodramatic; but the third type frequently encroaches on the first
two. The characters are mostly stereotypes: charming young
lovers, tyrannical parents, semi-Gothic villains, ingratiating prank-
sters, and diabolical women. There is very little psychological
realism and no genuine character development, although—predictably—we find some abruptly repentant scoundrels.[42] Like all
Hood's works, the stories maintain a rigorous moral purity; William Michael Rossetti, with characteristic delicacy, says that they

are "somewhat after the manner of Boccaccio (but how far different from his style may easily be surmised). . . ." [43] Hood's closest approach to a "suggestive" situation occurs in "The Chestnut Tree" when the Hidalgo's daughters are found to have "a brace of young comely gallants" hidden in their closets, but we are hastily assured that these are "gentlemen . . . and respecters of good manners" and "men of honour." [44]

The two volumes of *National Tales* were not well received by Hood's readers. Hood himself seems to have had some misgivings about the fate of the book, for the Preface certainly protests too much.[45] Perhaps the author's son, though understandably partial, was not entirely wrong in explaining the failure of both this book and *The Plea of the Midsummer Fairies* by "a reluctance on the part of the public to believe that one writer could produce both serious and comic works, or . . . a desire to extort the latter from him." [46] Later critics have, however, generally supported the reaction of Hood's public to *National Tales*, if they have not simply ignored the work or passed over it with a perfunctory note. Jerrold recalls some contemporary notices in which the book was "damned with faint praise as being good—in parts." [47] He himself asserts that, although the stories "show considerable invention," they "are, as a whole, the poorest books which Hood published." [48] He dislikes their "artificial style" and finds them so labored as to be "sometimes dull"; they are a failure because it was simply "foreign to [Hood's] nature to write romantic tales." [49] For Saintsbury, the *National Tales* "are not good for very much."[50] Paul Elmer More admits the justice of some of Hood's prefatory remarks but brands the book itself "a flat failure." [51] Brander dismisses the work with a reference to its "clogged narrative manner." [52] Reid, always as friendly to Hood as honesty allows, has virtually nothing good to say of the *National Tales*.[53]

Applied to the work as a whole, these strictures are justified; but not all the stories in *National Tales* are so bad as this chilling unanimity of critical opinion might imply. "The Spanish Tragedy" does achieve genuine suspense (at times), and "The Story of Michel Argenti" attains real pathos and horror; "The Eighth Sleeper of Ephesus" and "The Miracle of the Holy Hermit" are at least as entertaining as most of their kind; "The Owl" is a well told and appealing little exemplum; but perhaps the best of the tales is "The Fair Maid of Ludgate," [54] an unusual story of young love and filial loyalty set against the background of London during the plague. A happy ending is plucked out of the dreary horror, but not weakly or capriciously: the quality of love in the story is so steadfast that it gives vitality to life and demands its survival. Suspense is carefully sustained, so that only in the last sentence do we learn that Alice, her father, and the faithful Ralph have all come through their ordeal alive. The tale bears a remarkable atmospheric resemblance to some of Nathaniel Hawthorne's works in its re-creation of seventeenth-century town life and in its pervasive feeling of dread that seems to thicken the very air.

Although the critics are generally correct in their judgment that the two volumes of *National Tales* are among Hood's poorer publications, there is really nothing in them about which Hood's admirers need feel mortal embarrassment. Most of the tales do suffer to an extent from monotony of style and lack of force; but, taken in small doses, they can offer some pleasant reading. Some of the better ones would go well enough in a sizable anthology featuring stories of varied types.

III   Tylney Hall

In October of 1834—a hectic and exhausting year for Thomas Hood—appeared his *Tylney Hall,* a novel [55] in three volumes. Although the publication was far behind schedule, it is amazing that Hood was able to bring the book out as early as he did since it had to be written for the most part in moments stolen from his work on the *Comic Annuals* and on other projects. Hood was determined to produce a *magnum opus* that would establish him beyond question as a serious author, and *Tylney Hall* was launched with the highest hopes. Commercially, the book was successful (though not sufficiently to salvage Hood's wrecked finances); and it was reprinted many times. Artistically, the matter stood differently; and current reviews of the novel mixed censure with praise. Most of the criticisms—and the fact must have galled the author excruciatingly—were levied against the serious plot of the story; but the sheerly humorous and pathetic parts were generally appreciated.[56] Lamb's letter to Hood spoke for many of the critics, although more amiably than most: "I have been infinitely amused with 'Tylney Hall.' 'Tis a medley, without a confusion, of farce, melodrama, pantomime, comedy, punchery, what not?" [57] Much as Hood loved Lamb, it is doubtful that he was pleased by these words.

Hood himself acknowledged the reviews in his "Preface to the New Edition" (1840): "Of the reception of my first essay in the 'three volley line,' there was no reason to complain. The reviewers were generally kind and indulgent enough to have induced another attempt. Their strictures were mostly judicious, and were properly received with more patience than Sir Fretful Plagiary exhibited towards his critic. . . ." [58] Hood's words are amiable enough, but they are followed by thirty-seven lines of rather sharp rejoinder to one of the less cordial reviewers of *Tylney Hall.* [59] Hood's natural pleasure from the public's acceptance of his work must have been proportionately less than his disappointment from his failure to gain full recognition as a genuine novelist.

Critical opinion on *Tylney Hall* since the time of Hood has leaned toward the judgment pronounced by the severer critics of his day, for the novel is dismissed with a brief censorious note or a comment on the superiority of the rowdy humor and homely realism of some scenes to the stilted language and melodramatic actions of the main plot. [60] Close analysis of the story supports these findings, although, quantitatively, there are more good things in *Tylney Hall* than might be inferred from the available criticism. Whether or not these are worth pursuing through the book's 563 pages is another matter.

The story that flounders stubbornly through *Tylney Hall* may be summarized in a paragraph. Sir Mark Tyrrel, master of the Hall, adopts Walter, the Creole son of his brother Herbert, who has died after returning from the West Indies. Walter is befriended by a strange gypsy-like woman, Marguerite, who kindles his hatred against Ringwood and Raby, Sir Mark's sons. Through a diabolical scheme, Walter makes Raby the innocent cause of his brother's death; Raby flees the country and is later presumed a suicide. When Sir Mark dies of grief, Walter becomes master of Tylney Hall; but his triumph is blighted by his failure to win the hand of Grace Rivers, Raby's betrothed. Suddenly Marguerite informs Walter that she is really his mother, Indiana Thurot, and demands her rightful place as dowager of Tylney Hall. Rejected by her unfeeling son, she expires in convulsions. A short time later Walter himself is slain in a duel by Edward Somerville, a friend of the Tyrrels. Raby now appears, miraculously alive, to claim the hand of Grace and to restore honor and virtue to his father's estate. This summary takes no account of the comic episodes in *Tylney Hall,* which are frequent and sometimes quite long.

Clearly there is little originality of plot in Hood's novel.[61] The main literary influences on the work are easy to identify: the sentimental, picaresque, and Gothic novels of the eighteenth century. Situations and character types made current by Sterne, Fielding, and others are met at every turn in *Tylney Hall;* and Hood rarely equals his models. The novel can scarcely be said to have a structure at all, being episodic in the loosest sense of the word, jerky and fitful in movement, and highly digressive.

Occasionally Hood spoils what might have been a good descriptive passage or bit of action by sheer wordiness. It is nothing short of outrageous to spin a casual analogy into nearly three pages on the difficulties of presenting a pantomime.[62] On the other hand, the description of the preparations for the "rural jubilee" following this digression shows an agreeable union of comedy and realism—but even this is much too long. Hood's raillery at "fashionable" widows in Chapter XXXIII can be tolerated because it is both entertaining and perceptive, as when Hood concludes, "Finally, you may meet her at Brighton, fat, fair, and forty, telling you, with the comely cosy composure of a quakeress, that her heart is broken, she is tired of life, and her address is 10, Brunswick Terrace." [63] But even Hood's wit can hardly justify the sixty-six-line paragraph containing this sketch—the whole being devoted to a quite unnecessary defense of mixing sad and frivolous things in the same work. (Hood should have remembered that he was writing a novel and not a piece for the *Comic Annual.*) The death of Sir Mark is handled with commendable restraint in one brief paragraph,[64] but Hood then dissipates the effect with fifty lines of conventional moralizing. Over and over he insists upon spelling out reflections better left to the sensitive reader. This "dissociation of sensibility" is one of the fatal flaws of *Tylney Hall,* even though it is certainly due in part to the predilection of Hood's public for the sentimental and the didactic.

On the other hand, some parts of the plot show fairly competent handling. One instance is the use of an ambulatory conversation between Mr. Tablet (the mason) and a mysterious stranger to fill in the story after Ringwood's death.[65] As the quidnunc Tablet, pumped by the stranger, reveals the plot to send young Raby to

the gallows, suspense is built at the same time that the tempo of
the story is diminished; the conversational device also facilitates
our participation in the plot and introduces a refreshing shift in
viewpoint.[66] Furthermore, the account of Sir Mark's reaction to
Ringwood's death [67] shows a remarkable compression, both spatial
and emotional; it could well evoke the pity and terror of which
Aristotle speaks. In the pages following, the juxtaposing of the
ridiculous to the tragic, achieved through the bumbling prolixity
of Twigg and the tragicomic chaos of his household, makes for a
high degree of realism but also provides comic relief. Such comparative excellencies as these in *Tylney Hall* are too few to raise
the value of the whole, but they do deserve recognition.

As for Hood's characterization, even a cursory reading exposes
most of the major figures as unrelieved stereotypes. They never
really develop; for example, at the end of the book we are *told*
that Raby's hardships have added strength and hardihood to his
heretofore rather overdelicate temperament, but we are not *shown*
that they have. Still, one or two of the leading characters have at
least some individuality, or at least realism. One of these is
Thomas Twigg, the loquacious, bumptious, self-made "man of
property," inordinately proud of his rise from humble origins yet
bursting with determination to take his place in country society
with titled neighbors and liveried servants. Another is "Squire
Ned" Somerville, a hard-bitten, laconic, one-eyed, self-sufficient,
hardy individual who turns out to be a kind of rough-hewn knight
on a stout, if not white, horse—the redoubtable Barney. (Ned's
type is to appear again, though less fully realized and less appealing, in the American traveler of *Up the Rhine*.)

Walter Tyrrel, though devoid of real depth or complexity (he is
a Gothic villain *redivivus* or a degenerate Byronic hero), might
arouse some peripheral interest through his resemblance to
Shakespeare's Edmund in *King Lear*. This likeness could be the
subject of a separate article; here it is enough to note the following facts: Walter is of aristocratic blood sullied with the taint of
bastardy; he is sensitive, proud, and ambitious; he is a master of
guile, insinuation, and half-truth.[68] It is in this last-named characteristic that he most nearly resembles his Shakespearean kins-
man. Walter is, of course, not so colossally evil as Edmund: he
must have his wicked genius, "his female Mephistophiles," [69] who
seems slightly akin to Carathis in William Beckford's *Vathek*. It

might not be too imaginative to note an equivalence between Indiana Thurot, who undeniably resembles a primitive priestess, or
even a goddess of untamed nature, and the deity invoked by Edmund: "Thou, Nature, art my goddess. . . ." [70]

In his galaxy of minor characters Hood comes closest to real
distinction in *Tylney Hall*. Some of these are genuine fantastics
who inevitably recall the bizarre company created by Dickens—
who, be it noted, had not yet published a novel in 1834.[71] In many
ways, the most outstanding among this pathetic but fascinating
assemblage is "Unlucky Joe" Spiller, whose nickname is ill-suited
only on the side of understandment. He is "the mere foot-ball of
fortune," [72] what would now be called a "born loser." [73] That
Hood had a special feeling for Joe, whose role in the plot is not
important, is shown by the great amount of space allowed to the
ill-fated postillion. Reflecting on the persistent bad luck of Hood
himself, particularly in his business dealings, we might be par-
doned for theorizing that "Unlucky Joe" is the author's conscious
or unconscious self-caricature. But Joe is a viable character in his
own right, for a number of discriminating readers have felt his
strange and wistful appeal. Charles Lamb protested to Hood the
injustice of allowing a life of such unalleviated misery to culmi-
nate in a wretched death; [74] the *Athenaeum* review of *Tylney Hall*
singled out "Unlucky Joe" as a peculiarly sympathetic character; [75]
and later critics have found him specially interesting.[76]

Hood's attraction to "the insulted and the injured" is also shown
through his creation of "Tom in Tatters," who is almost as unfortunate as "Unlucky Joe," though he is less the victim of mere luck
or fate. Tom is the black sheep of the Tyrrel line, who, since his
expulsion from Oxford, has descended to the status of "town
drunk." At the same time, he is a scholar and a poet. But more
truly fantastic than either Tom or Joe is Uriah Bundy, shopkeeper
and seemingly half-demented Methodist parson, who is appro-
priately nicknamed "the Ranter." Huge, black-browed, scowling,
and savage, he is well rendered by Hood as a Cerberean com-
posite of the prophet, the bully, and the buffoon. While under the
spell of his vocation, "the Ranter" is a true fanatic whose single-
minded frenzy is never clouded by reason.

Among the less bizarre minor characters in *Tylney Hall* are
"Mrs. T.," the dowdy, fretful, light-minded wife of Thomas Twigg;
Tibbie, the garrulous Scottish maid; Constable Goff, whose com-

placent dim-wittedness makes him a worthy successor to Shake-speare's Dogberry; Jonas Hanway, proprietor of "The Rabbits," a typical stolid and sober English publican; Dr. Bellamy, or "Old Formality," the pompous, jargon-loving, obsequious physician, who makes us think of M. Homais in Gustave Flaubert's *Madame Bovary;* and Mr. Naylor (note the caractonym), the fawning, greedy, hypocritical undertaker. Needless to say, there is more than a little satire in some of these portrayals.

Most of what has been said of the characterization in *Tylney Hall* applies broadly to its language: Hood is at his poorest in those parts of the book meant to be serious and dignified on the grand scale; at his best in those depicting the comical and com-monplace. This contrast is seen especially in the dialogue. Some of the stilted sentimentality in the language of *Tylney Hall,* as in the scene where Kate Hamilton, Sir Mark's sister, adopts Grace as her daughter,[77] can be accepted as the inevitable product of Hood's day and, viewed tolerantly, might even have a quaint charm. The worst dialogue is found in the more specifically melo-dramatic scenes, where its faults are inextricably fused with those of character rendition. For example, it is hard to believe that a half-wild West Indian, even a high-born one like Indiana Thurot, would use phrases like "your myrmidons," "bare cope of heaven," "have my motives scrutinized," and "warning be more salutary." [78] One of the book's most colossal failures is the long dialogue be-tween Walter and his mother in Chapter XL.[79] Clearly, this en-counter between two satanic but somehow pitiful creatures, ending with the ghastly death of one, is meant to make our heads reel with its terrible grandeur. Yet no reader capable of a deep response to real tragedy (or, if the comparison is unfair, to the better melodramatic parts of Dickens) will be much moved. Throughout the story, the language of Walter Tyrrel and Indiana Thurot has failed to make them convincing characters, and now the characters make the language unconvincing.[80]

But Hood is not incapable of readable dialogue. His successes, like his failures, show the indissociability of character and lan-guage. The clumsy, well-meant efforts of "Squire Ned" and the Twiggs to comfort Sir Mark after the double funeral service for his sons are moving precisely because the people themselves *are* clumsy and well-meaning.[81] The light strokes of humor and satire in this scene serve only to humanize the tragedy and thus bring it closer to us. First tough, taciturn Ned brings Mark his favorite terrier, Nip:

"Don't want Nip?"
"Take him," answered Sir Mark.
They shook hands silently and slowly, during which process Ned fixed his one eye intently on the altered face of his old friend.
"Hold up!" he said, and, with these two syllables, he wheeled abruptly round and departed, without taking the least notice of any one else in the room.
It was now the Twiggs' turn, and they had evidently made up their minds to take a more elaborate leave than poor Ned's.

There now ensues a kind of alternating duet, almost in the vein of light opera or musical comedy, with Twigg advising Sir Mark and "Mrs. T." his sister. Kate is urged to "employ [her] mind" (in such activities as polishing furniture), to go visiting, to eat plenty (with a partiality to sweetbreads and good porter), to "have a good hearty cry," and to keep smelling salts handy. Thomas Twigg's reciprocating words of counsel to Sir Mark are of much the same cast, *mutatis mutandis;* for example: "If I was you, where I hunted one fox afore, I'd hunt two or three at once. That's the way, says you, to get rid of trouble." These samples can only sketch Hood's accomplishment in giving life to a humorous-pathetic conception of a scene through realistic dialogue; perhaps they may serve to lure a few readers into the work itself.

Other examples of true-to-life conversation in *Tylney Hall* are seen in the exchange between Kate Hamilton and Tibbie in Chapter XXIX [82] (or in practically any situation where Tibbie is present) and in the gossipy chitchat of Constable Goff, his "sub" Tippy, and Mat the gamekeeper in Chapter XXXVIII.[83] Unlike a large part of the picturesque dialogue in the novel, the last-named conversation helps to advance the plot (though probably not as rapidly as many readers would wish).

It was remarked some time back that Hood's readers and reviewers appreciated what Lamb called the "punchery" of *Tylney Hall* more than anything else in the book. We have had glimpses of this feature of the work, but in fairness to Hood one or two of his comic scenes must now be allowed full use of the stage. Far and away the most hilarious thing in *Tylney Hall* is the account in Chapter XXVIII of the "rural jubilee," or "grand to-do out of doors," staged by the socially ambitious Twiggs.[84] All goes wrong from the start, and the tragicomic climax comes when Daisy the cow breaks loose and makes a pitiful shambles of all the elaborate pastoral finery. She charges into the grand marquee, which half sags and half crashes to the ground; then, for an encore, she thunders through the greenhouse with Pompey, the black servant, clinging to her tail. Finally, nature herself, as if offended by such a gaudy mockery of rustic life, descends on the *fête champêtre* with a furious thunderstorm. The Twiggs can say, though hardly in the spirit of Prospero, "Our revels now are ended."

Another good comic scene, with the macabre touch so frequent in Hood, occurs when the Twigg family learns of Ringwood Tyrrel's death.[85] Twigg rushes to find a chair for his wife to swoon in, only to find that she has decided not to swoon. Meanwhile, Matilda, their daughter, is overcome by the "kicking hysterics"—although, we learn, "the young lady's grief was no greater than a fresh admirer would dissipate" (indeed, she and her mother have already selected a successor to Ringwood). Many more amusing tableaus await the reader willing to make his way through the novel. As to mere verbal wit, there is plenty of it in *Tylney Hall,* perhaps even too much; but this facet of Hood's talent need not be additionally explored at this time.

The trouble with *Tylney Hall* is, quite bluntly, that Hood was attempting something for which he had no real talent and indeed no real inclination. As will be seen in Chapter 6, he was right in believing that he could achieve something great as a serious writer; but he was wrong in his choice of a medium. Had Hood set his sights somewhat lower, he might have written a very acceptable half-burlesque, half-romantic novel of country life. But even in such a case he would have had to be more careful about structure, to have eliminated some of the word-plays, and to have concentrated on comic characters and situations. As it turned out, *Tylney Hall* was a mélange of disparate elements that Hood was never able to articulate successfully.

IV Up the Rhine *and* Our Family

The exhausting experience of writing *Tylney Hall* seems to have convinced Hood at the time that sustained novelistic narrative was not his forte; although he was to take to the genre once more with *Our Family.* His next major work in prose after *Tylney Hall,*

Up the Rhine (1840) [86]—the "German book" mentioned several times in Hood's correspondence—differed from *Tylney Hall* in almost every way imaginable; indeed, the Hood wit is about the only thing that the works had in common. *Up the Rhine* has been called an epistolary novel, mainly because it must be called something. Epistolary it most assuredly is; whether or not a work so shapeless and so inconclusive may rightly be called a novel is debatable. But novel or not, the work was extremely popular in its day: the first impression sold out, as Hood said, "in one short fortnight," [87] and a second edition was called for immediately.

Now Hood's "German book" is largely forgotten. Most literary histories do not mention it,[88] and even books and separata on Hood either follow suit or merely glance at the work in passing. Saintsbury calls *Up the Rhine* "the best of all the children of *Humphry Clinker*" and "a charming book," [89] but he does not analyze the work. Jerrold barely mentions the book and does not criticize it at all. Reid's thoughtful estimate of the merits and deficiencies of *Up the Rhine* [90] is the only criticism of its kind, and even it is quite brief.

Insofar as *Up the Rhine* has any structural pattern, it is, the author tells us, "constructed on the ground-plan of Humphrey [*sic*] Clinker, but with very inferior materials, and on a much humbler scale. I admire the old mansion too much," Hood continues, with becoming modesty and candor, "to think that any workmanship of mine could erect a house fit to stand in the same row." [91] Specifically, *Up the Rhine* is a kind of travelogue consisting of letters written by four travelers to their friends in England. The chief correspondent is Frank Somerville, a cultured and witty young man whose occasional enclosure of a poem or story attests to his literary bent; his uncle, Richard Orchard, an independent gentleman and self-styled invalid; Catherine Wilmot, Orchard's sister, a kind though rather muddleheaded lady—somewhat like "Chaucer's Prioress, who was 'all conscience and tender heart'" [92] —who punctuates her speeches with references to "poor George," her late husband; and Martha Penny, the group's Cockney maid. Their respective addressees are Gerard Brooke, Peter Bagster,[93] Margaret Wilmot (Catherine's sister-in-law), and Rebecca or "Becky" Page—none of whom is heard from directly. Some fellow voyagers are mentioned now and then, the most prominent being John Bowker, called "Redface" or "Pepper," a florid, testy, loquacious middle-class Englishman, and "Yellow-face," a laconic, unsociable, rather malicious American. The two are, of course, enemies from the start.

Hood's most signal achievement in *Up the Rhine* is the deftness with which he varies the style of each letter writer to match his character and temperament. This quality of the work is best illustrated through excerpts in which the different characters give their impressions of the same scene or incident, as in their accounts of a visit to the great cathedral in Cologne. Only a sentence or two of each is quoted: [94]

Martha: Colon is full of Sites. The principle is the Cathedrul, and by rites theres a Crane pearcht on the tiptop . . . but I was out of luck, or he was off a feeding, for he wasn't there.

Richard: I have seen the famous Cathedral, which is a fine building, and as such an uncomfortable sight, for it looks like a broken promise to God.

Frank: In looking upward along the tall slender columns which seem to have sprung spontaneously from the earth . . . I almost felt, as the architect must have done, that I had cast off the burden of the flesh, and had a tendency to mount skywards.

Catherine: I have said nothing of Cologne Cathedral . . . and instead of the Cathedral, I would rather have seen a certain village spire, rising above the trees, like a poplar turned into a steeple.

Martha is a type familiar to all—an *ingénue* in the literal sense, a kind of female Huck Finn with a Cockney accent. Frank is clearly a man of what we loosely call a "poetic" nature, though his main concern as a correspondent is usually to be wittily amusing. Richard, less sensitive than Frank, breezier and more matter-of-fact, is yet more perceptive and tolerant than we might expect of one of his class; certainly he is no Colonel Blimp. Catherine is very much the insular-minded tourist to whom everything foreign is, if not downright outlandish, "so very different" from the good old ways of home; her name is legion. We are not surprised to learn that this well-brought-up lady is shocked when the company is joined at lunch by *"a common soldier!"* [95] The matter is, however, viewed quite differently when Catherine learns that this young man is actually a Prussian baron discharging his military obligation: "The helping himself first, to a little wine, and then the officer, was only a customary politeness, in case there should be any dust or cork in the neck of the bottle." But Catherine is basically fair and sensible, for she admits her error and learns from it: "It will be a warning to me for the future not to be so rash in my judgment of foreigners, and foreign customs." [96]

The subject of insularity and prejudice is touched on several times in *Up the Rhine*. The *Memorials*, especially Hood's letters, show that he himself experienced these feelings and resisted them; and so do his characters: Richard finds the German students to be much like what we might now call "hippies," but he still shows some insight and tolerance; Frank, more truly sophisticated, and more thoughtful, generally shares his uncle's sentiments but is more aware of their complex implications. [97] As often happens in the book, Martha's remarks supply an amusing counterpoint to Frank's more profound observations. [98] Religious tolerance is also an occasional theme in *Up the Rhine*. Richard Orchard, although hardly a militant champion of Roman Catholicism or an apostate from the Church of England, argues at some length that the latter might profit by the example of the former in ministering to the old and needy; and Frank's friend Markham makes a long, impassioned speech on behalf of the Jews. [99]

Remarks like those in the preceding paragraphs must not be allowed to make *Up the Rhine* sound like a serious and tendentious book, for above all it is entertaining. Hood has by no means sworn off punning. At one joint in the journey a fine lady who prefers to stay inside her carriage on board ship is swept overboard (luckily she is saved). "Poor thing," says Catherine, "it's the nature of her bringing up." Richard agrees, but adds that "it's an unchristian bringing up that prepares one so badly for going down." [100] The rough seas continue, causing the ship to give "such an awful lurch," says Frank, "that I seriously thought we should be left in it." [101] Later, he writes so much about the wonders of Cologne that he suspects Gerard will find his letter "as long as an Eau de Cologne bottle without its spirit." [102] After a wretched night in Bonn, Frank complains that "a night in Bonn is anything but a bonne nuit!" [103] And his comment on the "toilsome expedients" of the vineyards is "Hic, labor, *Hock* opus est!" [104]

Nevertheless, a comparatively small portion of the fun in *Up the Rhine* is merely punnic; oftener it arises from such ridiculous situations as always occur in foreign travel. Some of these involve language problems, as in the case of the Englishwoman who keeps calling out "Hoof! Hoof!" and is quite put out that the *garçon* "doesn't even know the French for an egg!" [105] Then there is the dialogue in which Mrs. Markham tries very hard to tell the German servant that she wants a chicken. In desperation, the lady finally cries that she wants something " 'all covered with feathers —fathers—feeders—fedders!' 'Hah, hah!' cried the delighted German, at last getting hold of a catchword, 'Ja! ja! fedders—ja wohl!' and away went Gretel, and in half an hour returned with *a bundle of stationer's* quills!" [106] Another contretemps occurs when Richard falls ill and Catherine consults a German doctor, whose advice to "rob his chest" is distressingly misconstrued.[107]

In another humorous episode, the spirit of the trickster rules. Frank's Uncle Richard, an incorrigible *malade imaginaire* who really seems stout as a Trojan (he suffers only one indisposition on the trip, and even that is a subject for comedy), has told his lawyer that, if he fails to write home on schedule, he is to be "presumed dead." When Richard forgets to write from Rotterdam, Mr. Bagster informs Frank (for Richard's benefit) that his uncle's will is being probated. Frank perceives that the whole thing is "a plot got up between Bagster and Dr. Truby, by way of physic to a mind diseased." [108] The shrewdness of his guess is proved when Richard, with unusual vigor for an invalid, indignantly protests that the really insufferable injustice is his having been "made out a complete hypochondriac, which I never was in my life!" [109]— but his fundamental good nature soon reasserts itself.

Comedy of still another kind, one bordering on the slapstick— which, however, it escapes through the device of first-person narrative by the main figure in the incident—is seen in the "undelicate" situation that results when Martha's floating bath-house is struck by a barge: [110] "So out I run . . . jist as I was, with nothin on but my newdity; but decency's one thing, and death's another. . . . Luckily, none of the mail sects was passing by, for xcept won Waterloo blue bonnit, we were all in a naturalized state, like so menny Eves."

Before leaving *Up the Rhine*, we must note one more feature of the work—its picturesque descriptions, of which the following is a fair sample:

As you leave the open country around Bonn, the towns and villages become more retired in their habits, the natives creeping like earwigs and cockroaches into the cracks and crevices of the land, where their habitations are crowded into such narrow gorges and gulleys as to be only visible when you are right abreast of these ravines. You then discover a huddle of houses. . . . A church spire generally rises above the dark-clustered roofs; and a number of little chapels, like religious outposts, are perched on the neighbouring heights.[111]

Although light, Hood's *Up the Rhine* manages to be a very readable book without descending either to melodrama or to slapstick. Hood obviously exerts himself to entertain, but the work is more than a series of jokes, puns, and farcical situations. *Up the Rhine* has moments of genuine insight; the characterization is better than that in *National Tales* or (with one or two exceptions) in *Tylney Hall;* it contains some fine description. We would have to admit in the same breath that the book appears to have no real structure and hence no organic wholeness. The stories and poems sprinkled throughout the work serve no discernible structural purpose; they leave the impression of being "leftover" pieces that Hood was determined to use somehow (though they are brought in plausibly enough as effusions on the sites visited by the literary Frank). On the other hand, it could be argued—admittedly, with difficulty—that the looseness and inconclusiveness of the story are at least partly the result of a deliberate attempt to establish a symbolic equivalence between the river and the people traveling on it. The Rhine meanders and winds its way to final loss of identity in the infinite sea; so it is with the travelers, whether the sea be conceived as the world to which they return or as death. But we need not get so metaphysical about *Up the Rhine* to acknowledge it as a good work of its modest kind.

Not until he was almost literally on his deathbed did Hood cease to attempt to write a novel that would win discriminating critical acclaim as well as popularity. *Our Family,* his final effort, was not abandoned until February, 1845, about fourth months before the author's death. Twenty-three chapters were completed. In *Our Family,* Hood abandoned the epistolary technique of *Up the Rhine;* but, as the subtitle *A Domestic Novel* suggests, the new work was emphatically not a return to the manner of *Tylney Hall.*

The plot of *Our Family,* although slow in getting under way, carries us to a high pitch of interest and even excitement before it breaks off. The story begins with the birth of twin boys to "the doctor" and his wife (we never learn their surname—only the initial "B"). Everything is related from the viewpoint of one of the twins, Rumbold, who must have a truly remarkable memory. Tension develops when the amiable doctor becomes unpopular in his community, partly because he refuses to sell "opies" (laudanum pills) and partly because of a misunderstood remark by Kezia, his good-hearted but tactless maid. In a tragicomedy of errors, borrowed silver is stolen from the christening party, the doctor's wife squanders almost their last penny on a worthless lottery ticket, and the doctor is accused of "resurrecting" a child's body for his laboratory. (We strongly suspect that the guilty man is Dr. Shackle, the doctor's competitor, who is free with his "opies" and who steals his colleague's patients.) Forced to resign as parish doctor, the innocent hero has his home set upon by a furious mob that breaks his windows and burns him in effigy in his own yard. There is no more; and we are left to wonder forever about the fate of the worthy doctor and his family.

Our Family has interesting, down-to-earth characters. Foremost among them is the doctor himself, kind and generous, with an unquenchable sense of humor that saves him from being crushed by the stupidity of his neighbors. Others worth noting are Kezia, the maid, who has the outer homeliness and inner beauty of Flaubert's Félicité [112] but is much more talkative; Mrs. Prideaux, the prissy, "superior" nurse who is actually a highwayman's doxie; Postle, the doctor's assistant, dour and pedantic but honest and loyal; Dr. Shackle, who could be another Uriah Heep and an unredeemed Ebenezer Scrooge united in one person; Uncle Jinkins Rumbold, the eccentric and opinionated rich relation; and poor Catechism Jack, whose brains have been addled by a childhood accident. Quite noticeable is the Dickensian flavor of the names in *Our Family*: besides those just mentioned are found Poplitt, Bearcroft, Pegge, Peckover, Ruffy (or Ruffey), Noak, Spinks, Cobley, and Cropper. We remarked in the characters of *Tylney Hall* an anticipation of those in Dickens' novels. However, Dickens had published several of these by the time Hood began *Our Family*, and it is likely that here the influence—if there was influence—worked the other way.

Much humor is scattered throughout the pages of *Our Family*. There are, of course, the usual puns and witticisms. Of the larger humorous episodes, several are difficult to forget. In one, the doctor is able to improve the lot of a poor child in the community by an ingenious prescription for "poor dear darling Florio," a pet monkey belonging to the "great lady": [113] the ailing animal must be cuddled by a child's warm body and made to eat heartily and exercise regularly by imitating the child. Some good domestic comedy is created as the family argues over the naming of the twins, how many godparents they should have, and who these should be.[114] Realism and humorous exaggeration are nicely balanced in Rumbold's account of a severe verbal clash between Kezia and two old termagants, punctuated by Kezia's malapropisms and the doctor's gentle corrections.[115] Like most of the comic scenes in *Our Family*, all these have an admixture of pathos, sometimes of pain.

Since there has been relatively little critical comment on *Tylney Hall* and *Up the Rhine*, we are not surprised to discover even less about the fragmentary *Our Family*. The longest notation on the work is an eighteen-line paragraph by Brander,[116] who thinks that if the novel had been finished it would be the best of Hood's longer prose creations. If this be true, the reason is that it would have more organic wholeness and more of a genuine plot than *Up the Rhine* and more unity of tone, truth of language, and fullness of characterization than *Tylney Hall*. When all is said, we find in each of these earlier works (though especially in *Tylney Hall*) a shaky whole relieved by some good parts. Had Hood completed *Our Family*, possibly we would see, as in so many novels, a good whole marred by occasional blemishes.

CHAPTER 6

Poetry of Social Protest

IT is doubly fitting that the final chapter in a study of Thomas Hood should deal with his humanitarian poems, for this last expression of his poetic talent was also the one that was to bring him his most lasting fame. The most authoritative recent study of Hood sees him as practically the inventor of social-protest poetry,[1] at least for the Victorians and their successors. This view is not, as hasty judgment might surmise, an exaggerated one. Few readers will question Hood's primacy over Ebenezer Elliott, the "Corn-Law Rhymer," and other nearly forgotten petitioners in verse. But, some will ask, what of the great Romantics? Despite the passion, eloquence, and concern of these men, their efforts did not establish anything like a generic *kind* of humanitarian poetry; and very seldom did any of them produce verses that were recited in homes and schools and sung on the stage and in the streets as were some of Hood's. Furthermore, Hood's reputation and influence in this area were almost as strong in some other countries as in his own.[2]

I *Humanitarianism in Various Keys*

Even the earliest poems of Hood sometimes reveal his awareness of the plight of poor and neglected people—those constantly "put upon," whether by callous profiteers or by promoters of "progress." Among the more obvious examples of such poems are several in *Odes and Addresses to Great People* (1825): "A *Friendly* Address to Mrs. Fry *in* Newgate," "An Address to the Steam Washing Company," and "Ode to H. Bodkin, Esq."; and even the merrily mocking "Ode to Richard Martin, Esquire" concludes with a possible hint that Mr. Martin might give some thought to human as well as to brute sufferers. Occasionally, too, earlier poems that are not humanitarian in purpose anticipate some of the phrasing of the later protest poems. We may compare, for example, these two passages, the first from "Ode: Imitated from Horace" (1828) and the second from "The Song of the Shirt" (1843): "Oh! but to smell the woodbine sweet! / I think of cowslip cups . . ." (11. 25–27); "Oh! but to breathe the breath / Of the cowslip and primrose sweet" (11. 65–66).

Perhaps the first poem by Hood that clearly looks toward "The Song of the Shirt" and "The Lay of the Labourer" is the serio-comic "Answer to Pauper," printed in the *Athenaeum* in February, 1823.[3] The poem is signed "Overseer," and the terseness of the title itself suggests a graceless, cold-business attitude usually associated with that position. The content might strike us as a versified amplification of Scrooge's remark about the superfluousness of the poor in Dickens' *A Christmas Carol* ("If they would rather die . . . they had better do it, and decrease the surplus population"), especially when "Overseer" concludes "If such as you don't like this world—/ We'll pass you to the next." If Hood remains the jester here, it is as a "bitter fool" striving to pry open the eyelids of those who will not see.

Several pieces composed by Hood in the early or middle 1830's reveal through chinks in their humorous façades that Hood kept a rather tight finger on England's sociopolitical pulse. "A Charity Sermon" (1833) is a somewhat Burnsian monologue by a self-styled philanthropist who gets into much trouble through his benevolent acts: placing in an orphanage the child of the woman he has seduced, putting bad coins into beggars' hats, renting a ramshackle house to "ten motherless babes" (all of whom die when it collapses)—and so on. He is therefore "utterly done with Charity." The "Ode to Sir Andrew Agnew, Bart." (1834) reminds its subject—a fanatical Sabbatarian who proposed to increase church attendance by making all Sunday labor illegal—that "True religion need not be quack'd/ By an Un-merry Andrew!" (11. 41–42). These lines exemplify the fusion of the heartfelt and the jocular so often found in Hood. In the closing couplet, he advises "Un-merry Andrew" to "Read right this text, and do not further search/ To make a Sunday Workhouse of the Church." Although less powerful (because less personal), this poem has much in common with the "Ode to Rae Wilson," examined earlier.[4] It is akin also to the "Ode to J. S. Buckingham, Esq., M.P." (1835). James Silk Buckingham (who incidentally was founder of the *Athenaeum*) was such a zealous champion of temperance that he would have had all the public houses marked with skull and crossbones and all spirit-sellers in Belfast pensioned off.[5] Hood feared that in their fervor Sir James and his committee would forget

> *That men are brothers,*
> *And those who make a fuss*
> *About their Temperance thus,*
> *Are not so much more temperate than others.*
>
> (11. 299–302)

In both these "odes," Thomas Hood takes his stand for tolerance and common sense in coping with domestic problems: averse to impiety and insobriety alike, he shies away from a cure that threatens to be worse than the malady. His main point is that we cannot make men *want* to be better than they are by compulsive legislation. Hood was not a great thinker and never supposed himself one, but he did see that to treat the restive "lower classes" like disobedient children is to confuse symptom with disease—a truth that men have learned but imperfectly in our own century.

As Hood's career is traced from the late 1830's into the 1840's, many poems appear that are concerned more or less specifically with the plight of the workingman. Like nearly all the pieces considered in this chapter, except the half-dozen or so to be grouped with "The Song of the Shirt" and a very few others, these are externally on the comic side. "Agricultural Distress" (1837), a clever commentary on the Poor Law in the form of a kind of mock-eclogue, concludes that real "Hagricultural [*sic*] Distress" is not mere personal hardship but "the *Farming of the Poor!*" (1. 170). "The Assistant Draper's Petition" (1839) pleads for a quitting time of not later than seven o'clock for shopmen's helpers; Hood tenders his petition to prove "that they have rhyme, as well as reason, to offer in support of their resolution." [6] The pathos of this poem anticipates in less somber key that of "The Song of the Shirt." [7]

"The Sweep's Complaint" (1839) deserves comment about its form since it employs a device not hitherto seen in Hood's work. The poem has a thirty-two-line introduction consisting of four eight-line units run together without stanzaic division. The fourth and eighth lines are in iambic trimeter; the others are in iambic tetrameter; and each unit rhymes *aaabccccb*. This rather singsong pattern is followed, with comical abruptness, by the lines spoken by the Sweep himself, which are in the clattering, draggle-tailed couplets of the "Letter of Remonstrance" following the "Address to the Steam Washing Company": "Well, here's a pretty go! here's a Gagging Act, if ever there was a gagging!/ But I'm bound the members as silenced us, in doing it had plenty of magging" (11. 33–34). Protesting a recent act forbidding chimney sweepers to advertise by their traditional cry of "Sweep," the speaker wishes that black sweeps, like other black people, had their Wilberforce (11. 66–67). Again, Hood combines humor and pathos to awaken his readers to a genuine grievance.

During his career Hood wrote no wholly serious work dealing with England's Negro population. There is, however, at least a serious core to the prose piece "The Black and White Question," [8] and a few poems show that the matter was never far from Hood's thoughts. "The Doves and the Crows" (1839) is a picturesque, spirited, yet ironic song of celebration about the freeing of the slaves that stands out from other English and American poems about this subject chiefly because of its air of carefree camaraderie. Many readers might find the poem's language, or even its overall view of its subject, too painfully reminiscent of the Negroes' depressed way of life during the period of slavery and even long after. To some extent—the degree is impossible to ascertain—Hood must have sought this response. Presumably he meant to write a jubilant psalm in the spirit of the enfranchised people themselves but in such a way as to jab at the white reader's conscience:

> Come all ye sable little girls and boys,
>   Ye coal-black Brothers—Sooty Sisters, come!
> With kitty-katties make a joyful noise;
>   With snaky-snekies, and the Eboe drum!
> From this day forth your freedom is your own:
> *Play,* Sambo, play,—and Obadiah, groan!
>   (11. 1–6)

Some of the irony in the poem results from the fact that it was written as a mild satire on the Quakers' interest in Abolition ("Obadiah" is one of Hood's names for a Quaker in his foreword to the work).[9] However, the reader need not know this fact to feel the impact of the piece.

More fantastic, if no more truly imaginative, than "The Doves and the Crows" is "A Black Job" (1844), which is in the free style of Hood's comic odes. As a color-bar poem, "A Black Job" joins hands with many another work of Hood's day and of our own, but it is surely unlike any in the story it tells. The committee of a "Philanthropical Society" conceives the idea of rendering society a great service by scrubbing the black people white. Money for tubs, brushes, and soap is soon raised by public subscription; and these materials are put to energetic use. Still the Negroes are black. In the end, however, humanitarianism and science triumph over rebellious nature: "We mean to gild 'em!" (1. 234). Once more we must note that Hood's way of exposing the absurdity of color prejudice is out of fashion today—but no one can call it ineffective.

The convenient though admittedly vague term "Miscellaneous" must be summoned to embrace a fairly large group of poems—published mostly in *Hood's Own,* in the 1839 *Comic Annual,* and in *Whimsicalities*—that broadly reflect Hood's sensitivity to the restlessness permeating English society in his day. With a few exceptions, these pieces are on the humorous side. Among them are "A Plain Direction," "Verses Mistaken for an Incendiary Song," "Lines on the Celebration of Peace" (all 1839), "The University Feud," "Laying Down the Law," "The Lark and the Rook," "Party Spirit," "A Reflection on New Year's Eve," and "Epigram: On the Depreciated Money" (all 1844). Few of these poems need detain us long.[10]

"Lines on the Celebration of Peace," one of two "Quakers' Conversazione," stands out amid the works just named because of its impassioned tone and its vigorous use of simple, familiar rhetorical devices, especially personification and ironical interrogation.[11] Hood's ascription of the poem to "Dorcas Dove" perhaps misleads us to expect something light and whimsical. The idea that Peace should plug her ears or that "Captains should come like sucking Doves,/ With Olive Branches in their Bills" (11. 1–20) might seem on the burlesque or antic side, but these are genuine conceits and not mere *bons mots.* It is possible, but unnecessary, to see double entendre in "Bills"; the same is true of the connection that some might make between lines 19–20 and Bottom's "I will roar you as gently as any sucking dove. . . ."[12] The sympathy for the common soldier shown by Hood is something that he shares with several of the Romantics, such as Blake, Wordsworth, and Coleridge:[13]

> Lo! where the Soldier walks, alas!
>   With Scars received on foreign Grounds;
> Shall we consume in coloured Glass
>   The Oil that should be pour'd in Wounds?
>
> The bleeding Gaps of War to close,
>   Will whizzing Rocket-Flight avail?
> Will Squibs enliven Orphans' woes?
>   Or Crackers cheer the Widow's Tale?
>   (11. 29–36)

This poem is somewhat over-rhetorical, but pacifist poetry is almost certain to be so. The work does not lack power.

Another basically serious poem, though of a more whimsical species, is "The Lark and the Rook," one of Hood's several revivals of the allegorical beast-fable. Asked why, alone of all birds, the lark continuously soars and hovers, it replies that it cannot bear to settle on "scurf/ Of dirt and infamy" that men have spread upon the earth (11. 47–49). The "Moral" (so labeled) concludes the poem:

> Alas! how Nobles of another race
> Appointed to the bright and lofty way
> Too willingly descend to haunt a place
> Polluted by the deeds of Birds of Prey!

A second, and more humorous, beast-fable, "Laying Down the Law," seems to owe something to Burns ("The Twa Dogs") and perhaps to Swift ("The Beasts' Confession to the Priest"), but its immediate inspiration was a picture by Sir Edwin Landseer.[14] Not surprisingly, the poem turns out to be a satire on "the law's delay." A taint of bitterness intrudes toward the end of the work as the poet voices the doubtful hope that canine litigants may be better served by their laws than "poor Dogs" of "human suitors" are by theirs (11. 103–10). Here once more is the device of *ridentem dicere verum* so recurrent in Hood.

II Later Poems of Social Protest

All the intermittent but persistent flickers of social concern in Hood's poetry converge into a fairly steady flame of genuine protest poetry in the last two months of 1843 and in the first five of 1844. In the fall of 1843, things were going very badly indeed for Hood: his health was no better than usual, and he was out of a job and seemed unable to find one—an acceptable one at least.[15] The only way Hood could find the editorship that he needed was to create his own magazine, an almost impossible task in his circumstances and surely one fraught with great anxiety.

But during this period Hood wrote and published his most famous poem—a work that, as events were to prove, was no mere isolated curiosity. It is not so remarkable that his personal difficulties seem to have triggered a renewed creative effort: this phenomenon is rather common among artists. Especially interesting is the fact that in Hood's case this cathexis was directed not toward escapism or fantasy, as in the Freudian concept,[16] but toward a fuller understanding of, sympathy with, and involvement in the problems of everyday people. Misfortune can alienate one from the mainstream of life or draw him deeper into it; the recognition that for Hood it did the latter can help us to understand him better. As Walker has well said, "the true Hood . . . [was] neither a jester nor a denizen of fairyland, but a man deeply impressed with the realities of life." [17] Hood did not have to find, in Freud's phrase, "the way back to reality," for he never really left it.

At a most harrowing time, therefore, Hood began the series of poems that made his fame as a serious artist in his day and that for most readers and many critics sustain his reputation in ours. The first three of Hood's "public poems," as they are sometimes called, first appeared in the pages of *Punch*. The history of Hood's relationship with this publication is mildly amusing. *Punch* would appear to have been a made-to-order outlet for Hood's talent, but it got off on the wrong foot with him by printing in its premier issue (July 17, 1841) a facetious advertisement on behalf of "Mr. T. Hood, Professor of Punmanship." The joke was surely harmless enough and might even have been meant to invite Hood's contributions; but Hood was piqued; he was in no mood for jokes at his expense, especially one that confirmed his public image as a writer who never doffed his cap and bells. Eventually, however, he began contributing some minor pieces.

Contrary to a common impression, "The Song of the Shirt" was not the first of Hood's social-protest poems of 1843–1844. The fact is that the group got off to a rather lackluster start. "A Drop of Gin," published in the November, 1843, number of *Punch*, could not by any standards be called a good poem. Irregularly bouncy and breathless in movement, like some of the comic odes, it still purports to be a serious verse tract, sweeping into its net practically every existing cliché on the evils of drink except "demon rum"—and even this one is approximated by "the dram of Satan! the liquor of Sin!" (1. 11). The poem has some slapdash vitality, but the effect that Hood apparently aimed for is hamstrung by his scrambling of the rhetorically melodramatic and the grotesquely commonplace (he might have done better to sustain the latter tone, as Burns did in *The Jolly Beggars*). Here, and not only here, Hood simply failed to make up his mind how to treat the subject.

Only a month after "A Drop of Gin," Hood published anonymously a poem that was to treble the circulation of *Punch*,[18] make the words of Hood ring from the lips of thousands, and even inspire the epitaph on his memorial at Kensal Green: "He sang the Song of the Shirt." The work has been anthologized so frequently that its opening lines are familiar to countless readers who are unaware of any other poem by Hood:

> With fingers weary and worn,
>   With eyelids heavy and red,
> A Woman sat, in unwomanly rags,
>   Plying her needle and thread—
>   Stitch! stitch! stitch!
> In poverty, hunger, and dirt,
> And still with a voice of dolorous pitch
> She sang the 'Song of the Shirt!'

Like numerous protest poems of the nineteenth century, including some others by Hood, "The Song of the Shirt" was inspired by an actual instance of human suffering [19]—the arrest of a wretched woman, a seamstress named Biddell, for pawning allegedly stolen articles. During the investigation of her case, the terrible conditions in the "sweat-shops" were revealed in such a way as to move the press to action and thereby to stir violently the conscience of the public. The London *Times* was quick to print a strong editorial on the case, and *Punch* promptly followed suit. Hood, after reading of the incident, was moved to one of those incandescent states of mind that seem to make heightened feeling and artistic expression practically simultaneous.

Hood's son gave the following account of the composition of "The Song of the Shirt" and its reception by the public:

> In the Christmas number of "Punch" . . . appeared the famous "Song of the Shirt." It was, of course, inserted anonymously, but it ran through the land like wild-fire. . . . At last my father wrote to one of the daily papers and acknowledged it. . . . It was printed on cotton pocket-handkerchiefs for sale, and has met with the usual fate of all popular poems, having been parodied times without number. But what delighted, and yet touched, my father most deeply was, that the poor creatures to whose sorrows and sufferings he had given such eloquent voice, seemed to adopt its words as their own, by singing them about the streets to a rude air of their own adaptation.[20]

Our first thought might be that this account shows some pardonable exaggeration; the fact is that Tom Hood underestimated the sensation produced by his father's masterpiece.[21]

Hood's public had already been aroused by reading of the Biddell case in the press; and doubtless it was much discussed in homes, in public meeting places, and on the streets. "The Song of the Shirt" was a dramatic and emotional crystallization of public feeling that ran easily through the mind because of its rhymed and strongly rhythmic verses. Hood spoke for England's conscience. The public had long known of the sweatshops and must have had some idea of their *modus operandi,* but for the sake of mental peace it was better not to face the matter too directly. Hood's poem (and of course the articles in the *Times* and *Punch*) not only compelled awareness but made it fashionable, so to speak. Furthermore, having a tragic or sentimental story stylized in a poem or song enables people who are normally rather inarticulate and taciturn to express freely emotions that might otherwise remain under tight cover.

The preceding remarks take no specific account of the poetic qualities of "The Song of the Shirt" or of its value as poetry, our main concern here. Examining the techniques of Hood's poem, we probably notice first its strongly rhythmic and accentual qualities. These are achieved through the mixture of iambic and anapestic feet in carefully balanced trimeters and tetrameters and through the use of a powerful but irregular refrain, consisting generally [22] of three monosyllabic feet, in all but three [23] of its twelve [24] stanzas. The "Work—work—work" in five of the stanzas,[25] occurring in both the first and third lines of all but one,[26] clubs like a bludgeon; the "Stitch—stitch—stitch" of three others [27] jabs like a needle. Also, Hood makes good use of two devices—alliteration and assonance—which, as was noted early in this study,[28] are prominent in many of his lyrics. An example of the former is the repetition of *w* in the opening lines of stanza one (quoted above) and in the closing ones of stanza nine: "Before I knew the woes of want/ And the walk that cost a meal!" (11. 71–72). Among word combinations showing assonance are those in the closing lines of stanza three:

> Seam, and gusset, and band,
> Band, and gusset, and seam,
> Till over the buttons I fall asleep,
> And sew them on in a dream!
> (11. 21–24)

Besides the obvious echoes in the first two lines, there are the combinations "gusset"—"button," "seam"—"asleep," "over"—"sew," "fall"—"on," and "asleep"—"dream." All these features help to give "The Song of the Shirt" an appearance of cohesiveness and regularity. It is noteworthy, however, that no two of the stanzas are metrically identical. The poem is singable without being singsong.

The generalization just made holds true also for the rhymes in "The Song of the Shirt": though less diversified than the metrics, they show more variation than a first impression suggests. The fourth, sixth, ninth, tenth, and eleventh stanzas have the same scheme (*abcbdefe*), as do three, seven, and eight (*ababcded*); the others have individual rhyme patterns. This arrangement provides a well-proportioned rhymic structure, as can be shown by letting these three groups of stanzas be designated *A, B,* and *C,* respectively:

C	C	B	A	C	A	B	B	A	A	A	C
(1)	(2)	(3)	(4)	(5)	(6)	(7)	(8)	(9)	(10)	(11)	(12)

The uniform rhymes of stanzas nine, ten, and eleven help to produce a sustained level of utterance that carries the seamstress's monologue to a climax (although, as we shall see in a moment, Hood has another climactic trick up his sleeve). Had Hood not added stanza eleven after the poem's initial publication, as some readers wish, or had he placed it after the third or seventh stanza, as some others do, stanzas nine and ten would share a volitive force strengthened by a common rhyme scheme. Of course, this effect is not negated entirely by the addition.

Besides the use of refrain to unify the poem as a whole, two other repetitive devices not serving this specific purpose are worth noting in their own right. One of these is in the middle of stanza five:

> 'But why do I talk of Death
>   That Phantom of grisly bone,
> I hardly fear his terrible shape,
>   It seems so like my own—
>   It seems so like my own,
>   Because of the fasts I keep,
> Oh! God! that bread should be so dear,
>   And flesh and blood so cheap!
>   (ll. 33–40)

The repeating of the line "It seems so like my own" adds to the horror of these lines through a certain deliberative quality—as if the speaker, appalled by her own words, realizes that she has allowed a terrible truth to slip out, and repeats them with slow and awful conviction. Finally, one of the best repetitive contrivances in Hood's poetry, although a very simple one, is the extra line in the last stanza, which otherwise is virtually identical with the first: [29] "And still with a voice of dolorous pitch,/ Would that its tone could reach the Rich!—/ She sang this 'Song of the Shirt!'" The addition of the penultimate line creates a couplet that effects a final cresting of emphasis and jars the reader's sensibility with a twinge of compassion or remorse. Outside the bounds of the woman's song itself, yet comprehending it, the extra line delivers just the right amount of dramatic irony.

Little need be said of the speaker's language in "The Song of the Shirt" except that in its naturalness and simplicity it comes about as close as any well-known English poem to satisfying the Wordsworthian criterion of "the very language of men." [30] Hood allows his seamstress the use of practically no words that the real Mrs. Biddell would not have known. The reference to Mammon (l. 86) might seem an exception, although a devout working woman might easily remember the name from Matthew 6:24 if she were literate or from the church service if she were not. A more serious objection might be raised to "It's O! to be a slave/ Along with the barbarous Turk" (ll. 13–14). As a whole, however, the language of "The Song of the Shirt" seems quite "real."

The poem's figures of speech deserve special attention. Two of the more memorable are syllepses (or, in the broad sense, zeugmas): "It is not linen you're wearing out,/ But human creatures' lives!" (ll. 27–28); "Sewing at once with a double thread,/ A Shroud as well as a Shirt" (ll. 31–32). There is an extraordinary rightness about these figures: they speak stark truth in the plainest language and yet show a genuinely poetic fusion of ideas—a common phenomenon enough, as when a ditchdigger exclaims "Sometimes I feel like I'm diggin' my own grave!" "The commonest man," says Keats, "shows a grace in his quarrel"; [31] and the principle may be extended to other states of heightened feeling (which is Keats's point).

Personification, sometimes laced with irony, is used several times in the "Song":

> And a wall so blank, my shadow I thank
> For sometimes falling there!
>
> (ll. 47–48)

> While underneath the eaves
> The brooding swallows cling
> As if to show me their sunny backs
> And twit me with the spring.
>
> (ll. 61–64)

> My tears must stop, for every drop
> Hinders needle and thread!'
>
> (ll. 79–80)

As the seamstress sings the first of these passages, perhaps we are to visualize her mask of sorrow as disturbed briefly by the hint of a smile; ironic realization is humor's grim cousin. (By the time of the "Song," Hood was an old hand at showing how irony bridges comedy and tragedy.) The idea of thanking one's shadow is grotesquely comical—it suggests something that Charlie Chaplin might do; yet the thought of loneliness so complete as to make one grateful for a shadow's company is ineffably sad. The second example is unforgettable mainly because of the phrase "twit me with the spring." "Twit" gives a much richer texture than could another word—say "chide"—for several reasons: it is an onomotope that produces a synaesthetic response; it is a punnic word with two meanings, both apposite in the context; it has a certain jaunty flavor, suggesting that even the poor seamstress once knew "youthful jollity" (so that her present case seems all the sadder).

The passage as a whole, together with the following stanza, reveals the singer as a person of genuine sensibility: one whose idea of a better world is neither the music hall nor the *haut monde* but rather a simple pastoral vision not devoid of esthetic value. Her words on the swallows show a sensitivity to nature that accentuates the idea of "common worth" without straining credibility. The third passage may of course be taken literally, but some would say that the tears hindering the singer's work represent a dimension of her being wholly at variance with the dull and dreary thing that her life has become.

A simple but telling use of metonymy apears in "the walk that costs a meal" (1. 72). Again, the words are simple and authentic —indeed, they could not be more so; yet, while making no claim to depth or complexity of thought, they have the compression and suggestiveness of true poetry. In this single respect, the passage would be difficult to surpass. To *explain* the connection of ideas in the line would require a good many words (the walk is not *literally* the price of the meal, and so on), but there is no need; we understand the figure at once, just as we do Milton's "Blind mouths." [32]

As Pope says, no poem is faultness; [33] and we must not be too disappointed to find the last figure of speech in "The Song of the Shirt" far less satisfying than those just noted. It occurs in the controversial eleventh stanza: [34]

> Seam, and gusset, and band,
> Band, and gusset, and seam,
>> Work, work, work,
> Like the Engine that works by Steam!
>
> A mere machine of iron and wood
>> That toils for Mammon's sake—
> Without a brain to ponder and craze
> Or a heart to feel—and break!
>>>> (11. 81–88)

There is something to be said for Hood's simile: it does contain pathos, and there is a certain appropriateness in his likening of the sweatshop laborer to an industrial machine. The effect might be vitiated, however, as we make the more apposite comparison between the machine and the wretched factory worker of the period, so that someone else claims a share of our sympathy at the very moment when the poet wants it to be concentrated on his subject. Some readers might object to the simile on more purely esthetic grounds, finding it labored, unauthentic, and even trite. It has been noted that stanza eleven was an afterthought, and perhaps Hood should have let well enough alone. "The Song of the Shirt" was the result of almost simultaneous inspiration and execution, and sometimes such a work is hurt as much by re-vamping as a less spontaneous one (like Milton's "Lycidas") is helped by it.

We have commented on the degree of realism and simplicity of language generally maintained in "The Song of the Shirt." It is perhaps superfluous to point out how vital these characteristics are to the portrayal of scene; yet some particulars must be ex-amined. The description of the seamstress herself in the first stanza, though not minute, is "real" enough to satisfy any reader: Hood has selected a few stark details and presented them in very plain words. With the possible exception of "dolorous," his phras-ing is as unadorned as the woman's own; he avoids any appear-ance of condescension toward his subject. The poet-persona only frames the scene with the first and last stanzas, letting the seam-stress speak for herself. Picture and frame fit as she describes her quarters much as she herself has been described—with enough detail to suggest the whole but not so much as to over-localize or distract: "That shatter'd roof,—and this naked floor—/ A table—a broken chair—" (11. 46–47). (We note how the brokenness of the lines parallels the idea of "shatter'd" and "broken.") The wom-an's recurrent references to her needle and thread and to parts of the garment that she is sewing help to keep before us the picture of a woman singing *as* she works, not just *about* her work (there would be no time for that). The literalist who protests that no worker as miserable as this one would be singing at all should be advised to flip through the pages of any folksong anthology. Surely the ancient tradition of the work song or chant, full of sad complaint, must have been in Hood's thoughts when he wrote this poem. It is plain that Hood powerfully *felt* the situation that is revealed in "The Song of the Shirt," and this fact saved the piece from the banality, and we are tempted to add from the orotund fakery so common in humanitarian poetry.

"The Song of the Shirt" was not Hood's only public poem in the Christmas, 1843, issue of *Punch*. Rubbing shoulders with it was "The Pauper's Christmas Carol," a piece in quite a different key; indeed, the two poems have practically nothing in common except humanitarian purpose. The third of the nine uniform stanzas of "The Pauper's Christmas Carol" best conveys the spirit of the work:

> 'Fed upon the coarsest fare
> Three hundred days and sixty-four
> But for one on viands rare,
> Just as if I wasn't poor!
> Ought not I to bless my stars,
> Warden, clerk, and overseer?
> Heigho!
> I hardly know—
> Christmas comes but once a year.
> (ll. 19–27)

It is easy to see why this poem was almost ignored in the tumult that greeted "The Song of the Shirt," and no one would call it great as either poetry or polemics. Critics have taken no significant notice of "The Pauper's Christmas Carol." Still, there are some good things in it: phrasing, meter, and rhyme are deftly handled on the whole; and the refrain, which keeps repeating the familiar words about Christmas from a quite unfamiliar viewpoint, uses cumulative irony to good effect (much as in "A Plain Direction"). There is no conventional sentimentality in the piece, and yet genuine pathos is achieved by juxtaposing the speaker's rueful awareness that the Yuletide feast signifies no real change in his condition with his determination to make merry while he can—once a year is better than not at all! The poem is essentially a fling at "do-gooders" who make a great thing of giving paupers a fine Christmas dinner but show no continuing concern over their problem; and the poem decidedly makes this point, one not barren of instruction for our own time.

Hood attempted to follow up "The Song of the Shirt" with several other poems of the same general kind printed in *Hood's Monthly Magazine*. "The Lady's Dream," "The Workhouse Clock," and "The Bridge of Sighs" appeared in fairly rapid succession between February and May, 1844; later in the year (November) came "The Lay of the Labourer." Hood also published other pieces in his magazine, and occasionally in *Punch*, in the early months of 1844. This record of work is impressive when we remember that Hood's health was so poor that, without the help of friends, his magazine could not have continued publication and that, in spite of Hood's popular success, his finances were again in crisis through his seemingly fatal bad luck in choosing publishers and proprietors.

Except for a trimeter in the first line, "The Lady's Dream" follows the Coleridgean form of "The Sea-Spell," "The Last Man," "The Dream of Eugene Aram," and "The Elm Tree." The poem is essentially a reworking of "The Song of the Shirt" using the dream motif so common in Hood, and as such it forces the comparison with its illustrious predecessor. Hood's compassionate and chivalrous feelings toward women enslaved by an economic machine were too strong to be contained in one poem (the addition of stanza eleven to "The Song of the Shirt" is one proof of the fact). "The Lady's Dream" caught, we might say, some of the overflow. Hood must be praised for his sensitive humanity; nevertheless, the harsh truth is that in "The Lady's Dream" he is plagiarizing himself—and not very successfully. Technically, the piece shows Hood's usual competence, though by no means at its highest level; the style and treatment are decidedly mediocre.

In the poem, a wealthy, pampered lady dreams that she is haunted by the ghosts of

> those maidens young
> Who wrought in that dreary room,
> With figures drooping and spectres thin,
> And cheeks without a bloom;—
> And the Voice that cried, "For the pomp of pride,
> We haste to an early tomb!"
>
> (11. 25–30)

In a less inflated work, the first four lines just quoted might evoke compassion (even though they echo "The Song of the Shirt"). But "pomp and pride" is itself rather pompous, or at least declamatory; and the repetition of these words in the line following this stanza is not one of Hood's better uses of this device. "Afric slaves" and "yonder cypress waves" (11. 32, 34) seem unnatural uses for un-

lettered seamstresses (or even for their ghosts). Elsewhere, "A
sad and sickening show" (1. 40) seems almost bathetic following
"I never saw/ A ground so full of graves," "And still the coffins
came," "Coffin after coffin still" (11. 36, 37, 39). "Of the many,
many troubles of life/ That grieve this earthly ball" (11. 45–46)
suggests the laureate of the home-town newspaper. The lady's
expression of remorse, which comprises the bulk of the piece, is
far too long and rhetorical. The simple and direct words that open
the final stanza promise to redeem the work somewhat:

> She clasp'd her fervent hands,
> And the tears began to stream;
> Large, and bitter, and fast they fell,
> Remorse was so extreme:
> And yet, oh yet, that many a Dame
> Would dream the Lady's Dream!

But the flatness of the fourth line nearly spoils all: after the Lady's
nearly eighty lines of monologue, we surely need not be *told why*
she is weeping. The volitive construction in the last two lines
sounds weak and overrhetorical beside that in the penultimate
line of "The Song of the Shirt." The "yet, oh yet," like other weak
repetitions in the poem, reminds us that Hood often betrays
through this mannerism a failure of inspiration even when his
humane feelings are strong and pure.

A comparison of "The Lady's Dream" and "The Song of the
Shirt" tells us much of Hood's capabilities and of his limitations.
There is an unsteadiness about his talent as a serious writer. In
the wide gap between a good and a comparatively poor treatment
of a theme from "common life," Hood again recalls Wordsworth—
although, generally, Hood's failure is less dismal just as his success
is less brilliant. Both poets at times confuse the expression of
sincere feeling per se with genuine poetic utterance.

"The Workhouse Clock" is a much better poem than "The
Lady's Dream" and has more originality, even, than "The Song of
the Shirt." The poem is composed of seven stanzas ranging in
length from eight to twenty-one tetrameter and trimeter lines—
the combination so often preferred by Hood. The feet are mainly
iambic, but there are more initial and terminal trochees than
might be expected. The rhyme is strong but irregular in pattern.

"The Workhouse Clock" describes a turbulent but purposeful and unidirectional mob on the move; and the mingling of the normal and the regular with the asymmetrical and the abrupt in the form of the work successfully projects the character of this mass movement. The feeling that we are actually watching a tumultuous stream of humanity surging through the streets of London is strengthened by the poet's naming of specific places progressively reached—Whitechapel, Cornhill, the Poultry, Ludgate Mart. Yet this mob is a symbolic and not a real one—for "The Workhouse Clock" is another of Hood's vision poems. His mixing of the commonplace with the quasimythic gives this poem a quality at once eerie and apocalyptic that is reminiscent of Blake.

The sweeping, tidal movement of "The Workhouse Clock" can be imparted only by substantial quotation:

> Who does not see them sally
> From mill, and garret, and room,
> In lane, and court and alley,
> From homes in poverty's lowest valley,
> Furnished with shuttle and loom—
> Poor slaves of Civilization's galley—
> And in the road and footways rally,
> As if for the Day of Doom?
> Some, of hardly human form,
> Stunted, crooked, and crippled by toil;
> Dingy with dust and smoke and oil,
> And smirch'd besides with vicious soil,
> Clustering, mustering, all in a swarm.
>   (11. 17–29)

Lines 26–29, richly textured with hard consonants, liquids and sibilants to suggest the multiformity of the throng's composition and movement, read especially well.

The destination of the westward-swarming mass of people described by Hood is the workhouse itself, where all suddenly stop and stand as one, with eyes "Upturned to the Workhouse Clock!" (1. 76). The poem ends with the fervent wish

> that the Parish Powers,
> Who regulate Labour's hours,
> The daily amount of human trial,

> Weariness, pain, and self-denial,
> Would turn from the artificial dial
> That striketh ten or eleven,
> And go, for once, by that older one
> That stands in the light of Nature's sun,
> And takes its time from Heaven!

Flowing where "The Lady's Dream" merely eddies, "The Work-house Clock" has a logical and vigorous thematic structure that on the whole justifies this rather didactic conclusion. Some readers might wish that Hood had ended the poem at line 76 and allowed them to *infer* the message of the final stanza—that parish authorities should shorten the hours of workhouse laborers. Possibly "The Workhouse Clock" would have been a better poem this way; but, as is usual in the writing of public poetry, the author would rather compromise his artistic ideals somewhat than to risk loss of communication with even one reader.

In Hood's next humanitarian poem, "The Bridge of Sighs," sometimes called his greatest, he returned to the subject of an unfortunate woman crushed by the toils of a modern slave system. The inferiority of "The Lady's Dream" to "The Song of the Shirt" suggests that, although Hood's indignation toward the sweatshops had not abated, he had gone as far as he could in the direction indicated by his first triumph as a public poet. What he needed was another specific jolt on his sensibilities to set off a new creative effort, and this seems to have been provided by the case of a young woman sentenced to deportation for the murder of her illegitimate baby followed by an attempt at suicide.[35] Humanitarians of the day saw her crime as the product of dehumanizing socioeconomic conditions, and the case was widely publicized.

"The Bridge of Sighs" has the most unusual form of all the poems in the present group; at first glance it gives the impression of novelty:

> One more Unfortunate,
> Weary of breath,
> Rashly importunate,
> Gone to her death!
> Take her up tenderly,
> Lift her with care;

> Fashion'd so slenderly,
> Young, and so fair!
> (ll. 1–8)

Hood's familiar tetrameters and trimeters have been discarded in favor of a dimeter line that is predominantly dactyllic. Approximately 42 percent of the lines are in straight dactyllic dimeter; there are also recurring combinations of a dactyl and a trochee, a trochee and an iamb, an iamb and an anapest, two amphibrachs, and others. Actually the poem has only three metrically identical stanzas. Hood thus follows his common practice of maintaining control through a dominant measure while avoiding monotony through variation. Similarly, the stanzas differ greatly in length, from four to nine lines, in the pattern 4-4-6-6-6-4-5-7-6-7-7-9-8-4-6-5-8-4. Diversity is seen also in the rhyme: there are nine patterns, the most common being *abab* and *aabccb*, used five and four times respectively; two others occur twice each and five only once each.

In "The Bridge of Sighs," Hood's adroit use of rhymic and metrical variation makes possible modulations of rhythm to reflect shifting nuances of attitude and feeling. Still, he has done a risky thing in writing a highly pathetic lyric of 106 lines in dimeters, and not every reader will think that he has succeeded. Critical opinion has been more sharply divided on "The Bridge of Sighs" than on any other of Hood's lyrics. Nineteenth-century critics before Saintsbury generally agree that it is a fine poem—possibly Hood's greatest. Jerrold quotes Browning as considering the piece "alone in its generation"; [36] Thackeray says " 'The Bridge of Sighs' was his Corunna, his heights of Abraham—sickly, weak, wounded, he fell in the full blaze and flame of that great victory." [37] Saintsbury, however, objects to Thackeray's encomium, complaining that this poem, like its famous companion "The Song of the Shirt," "seems . . . to be vitiated not only by some literary mannerisms, but by a certain sentimentality which is very apparent in much of the writing of that particular day. . . ." [38] Although he calls "The Bridge of Sighs" a "greater poem" than "The Song of the Shirt," he thinks its length even more excessive. While conceding that the work has "remarkable metrical beauty," Saintsbury accuses the author of sacrificing meaning to "metrical and other effects" (what these are he does not say) and of abusing the pathetic fallacy.[39] But the critic softens the effect of his words by admitting that "to say this is to say little more than that Hood is not Shakespeare," and he praises Hood's humanitarianism for having "not a streak in it of . . . maudlin sympathy with crime." [40]

Two critics writing about twenty years after Saintsbury,[41] Walker and Elton, clearly disagree with each other on the merits of "The Bridge of Sighs." Walker, unlike Saintsbury, finds it "never sentimental" but "Full of sentiment." Making the inevitable comparisons between this poem and the "Song of the Shirt," Walker judges the former to be "perhaps rather the finer of the two." [42] Elton, much to the contrary, thinks "The Song of the Shirt" "a far better piece" and is very hard on "The Bridge of Sighs," calling its treatment "bad," its dactyllic rhythm "jarring" and "tuneless," and some of its phrasing "grotesque." He acknowledges the author's sincere humanity, but he regrets that this very trait was an obstacle to his art, "as so often happens." [43]

Later scholars, perhaps less fearful than Saintsbury and Elton of being ranged with the Victorian sentimentalists, have usually praised "The Bridge of Sighs" not only for its humane compassion but for its lyrical excellencies. At the same time, they realize that it is not easy to separate the effects of these two qualities: Chew says, for example, that we find in "The Bridge of Sighs" "pathos redeemed from mawkishness by sincerity." [44] For Pritchett, both of Hood's great humanitarian poems are metrically brilliant; and he can discern no flaw in the later of them except a few "lines of self-parody" [45]—a fault that even the greatest poets have not always escaped. Hood's "the rarity/Of Christian charity" (11. 43–44) is admittedly bad; but to put the matter in perspective we might note that "with hand so various/Or might I say contrarious" was written not by Ogden Nash but by John Milton.[46] Brander speaks for many readers who consider "The Bridge of Sighs" the best of Hood's later lyrics.[47] Reid, in a sensitive discussion of the piece, finds that, despite some rather glaring faults, it has genuine power and lasting value deriving from the authenticity of Hood's human sympathies (*pace* Elton) supported by his metrical skill and his sense of what is perdurable in language.[48]

Only a very lenient judge would discover no lapses of taste and usage in "The Bridge of Sighs." At least one whole stanza, perhaps two, should never have been passed by the editor. The sixth stanza combines the faults of triteness, awkward usage, and poor taste to a degree hardly exceeded by the most deplorable passages in Leigh Hunt:

> Still, for all slips of hers,
> One of Eve's family—
> Wipe those poor lips of hers
> Oozing so clammily.
>
> (11. 27–30)

"Still" and "slips" have a conversational casualness unsuited to the occasion; "slips," with its (for once in Hood) unintended suggestion of a pun on the manner of the girl's death ("slipping" into the river), is especially unfortunate. The trite phrase "One of Eve's family" apparently seeks to mitigate the victim's sin by ascribing it to the ancestral weakness of womankind; Hood would do better to base his appeal for charity on more relevant and immediate grounds. Moreover, "for" fails to establish a satisfactory causal relationship between the ideas in the two pairs of lines. Finally, for many readers the last two lines elicit less pity than horror and disgust. Stanza nine is much too didactic:

> Alas! for the rarity
> Of Christian charity
> Under the sun!
> Oh! it was pitiful!
> Near a whole city full,
> Home she had none!
>
> (11. 43–48)

Hood's sermonizing is unnecessary, even for the dullest reader; the poem as a whole shows eloquently that the girl's case is pitiful and that Christian principles are more mouthed than practiced. (Incidentally, the quasi-Byronic rhyme "pitiful"–"city full" does nothing for the stanza.) Here, as in other instances, Hood might have underestimated his powers; or perhaps he was too submissive to current taste and practice. The charge of needless didacticism could be raised again over lines 76–79, which also, like lines 29–30 above, strike a physically repugnant note ("Lave in it, drink of it")—and this at the very moment when Hood wants us to feel *moral* disgust toward the girl's seducer.

Yet there would be no point in criticizing "The Bridge of Sighs" for its flaws were it not on the whole a very meritorious work: "Who breaks a butterfly upon a wheel?" [49] We have already glanced at the major aspects of the poem's mechanics, which of course must be kept in mind in examining its other features. Chief among these is the dramatic framework, which creates the picture of a small crowd of shocked and sorrowful people grouped like figures from the cast of a tragedy around the body of the girl as it is slowly taken from the water. Thus the scene is invested from the beginning with a solemn and ceremonial quality that gives it dignity and significance, and the short lines with their falling cadences produce a chorus-like chant that enhances the effect and helps universalize the scene.

At the same time, we are not spared the details of the actual contemporary event: the slender, fair girl with "garments/Clinging like cerements" (11. 9–10),[50] which drip constantly; her "fair auburn tresses" in streaming disarray (11. 31–33); the shimmering watery reflections from lighted windows and casements (11. 56–59); and "the dark arch" over "the black flowing river" (11. 65–66). The *particular* tragedy can easily be visualized, but without hard, limiting edges: it could be placed in sixteenth-century Venice or twentieth-century Chicago as readily as in nineteenth-century London. The iconography of the poem is such that it portrays movingly the specific tragedy and yet raises it to the level of the timeless and symbolic.

On this ground, it appears that those who have judged "The Bridge of Sighs" to be a better poem than "The Song of the Shirt" are in a strong position. (This is not to say, of course, that the latter poem is devoid of universal qualities or that it is inferior in all respects to the former.) Since the time of Thomas Hood, Western civilization has gone a long way—though not yet the whole way—toward eliminating the kind of tragedy described in "The Song of the Shirt." The sorrows of "The Bridge of Sighs"—the pitiful vulnerability of humankind, loneliness, despair—are still with us and probably always will be: the causes may change, but the consequences are the same. And, since Hood did not limit meaning by specifying cause, "The Bridge of Sighs" will always speak to men of the tears for things and of the mortal events that touch the soul.[51]

If it be tentatively postulated that "The Bridge of Sighs" is Hood's supreme effort as a public poet, is it also his greatest lyric outside this area? Its strongest competitor would surely be "Fair Ines." [52] This piece has many excellencies and none of the faults of "The Bridge of Sighs"—but champions of the latter will demur that it represents the maximal exertion of Hood's talent; that this is proved partly by its technical subtleties but above all by its intense feeling; that the great imperfect work must always be placed over the near-great perfect one. We are close here to the Racine-versus-Shakespeare type of controversy, which is seldom profitable because each side wants the other to accept as postulates what are in fact conclusions. It is doubtful that valid comparative judgments can be made between two lyrics of high quality unless they are very similar in subject and in the approach to this subject.

The last of Hood's humanitarian poems, "The Lay of the Labourer," was provoked by an incident that was literally to haunt the poet almost to the day of his death.[53] This, the case of young Gifford White, was described by Hood himself as follows:

In the spring of the present year this very unfortunate and very young man was indicted, at the Huntingdon Assizes, for throwing the following letter, addressed . . . to the Farmers of Bluntisham, Hunts, into a strawyard:—

"We are determined to set fire to the whole of this place, if you don't set us to work, and burn you in your beds, if there is not an alteration. What do you think the young men are to do if you don't set them to work? They must do something. The fact is, we cannot go on any longer. We must commit robbery, and every thing that is contrary to your wish.

"I am,
"An Enemy."

For this offence, admitted by his plea, the prisoner, aged eighteen, was sentenced . . . to Transportation for Life! [54]

In the November, 1844, issue of *Hood's Monthly Magazine* the indignant poet gave to the world "The Lay of the Labourer." The poem is incorporated in a prose sketch showing a group of ragged but respectable farm workers talking over their plight in a cheerless country alehouse (where they are reduced to drinking water). The informal meeting ends with the laborers singing their "chant," which is of course the poem itself. But Hood was far from finished with the Gifford White case. He followed his poem with a long, impassioned plea in prose on behalf of all laborers and of White in particular. Like Lord Byron in his speech on the "Frame-breakers," Hood indicated that harsh severity toward "a starving and desperate populace" is not an effective way to deal with its grievances: "One thing is certain. These are not times for visiting with severity the offences of the labouring poor, a class who, it is admitted by all parties, have borne the severest trials that can afflict the soul and body of man, with an exemplary fortitude and a patience almost superhuman." [55]

Not satisfied with pleading to his public, who would be moved to feeling but not necessarily to efficacious action, Hood wrote the Home Secretary himself, enclosing a copy of the magazine containing the poem and the appeal. Home Secretary Sir James Graham replied, as the poet's son put it, with "a few inches of red tape": [56] "Sir James Graham presents his compliments to Mr. Hood, and begs to acknowledge the Magazine accompanying his letter of the 30th instant." [57] We cannot wonder that Hood later characterized Sir James as "a cold, hard man, bigoted to the New Poor Law." [58] Fortunately, the public's reception of the "Lay" was more encouraging, as Hood remarked in a letter to his friend Dr. Elliot: "The 'Labourer' has made a great hit, and gone through most of the papers like the 'Song of the Shirt.' " [59] In spite of this success, the poem had failed in its immediate purpose. How much influence this and Hood's other public poems had in creating the indignation and concern from which reform must rise cannot, of course, be determined. [60]

Poems of social protest usually enjoy little acclaim or even remembrance after their age is past, but Hood's "The Song of the Shirt" and Mrs. Browning's "The Cry of the Children" are clearly exceptions. "The Lay of the Labourer" is now so little noticed that it is seldom discussed at any length even in studies of Hood—a regrettable fact, for the poem is powerful in its way. Technically, it strongly suggests the "Song," with which it shares these marks: almost identical length (the "Lay" is longer by a line); an eight-line stanza, with one exception (the third stanza of the "Lay" has ten lines); a mixture of iambic and anapestic feet in trimeter and tetrameter lines, with slight metrical variations among the stanzas; a rhyme scheme of *ababcded* or *abcbdefe*; [61] and a heavily accented refrain or semi-refrain ("A spade! a rake! a hoe!/A pickaxe, or a bill!" occurs in the first, fifth, and eleventh stanzas of the "Lay").

The language of "The Lay of the Labourer" equals or surpasses that of "The Song of the Shirt" in directness and simplicity, though not (needless to say) in emotional quality. There are very few phrases that might be boggled at as "literary," and even these are easily justified. Reviewing nineteenth-century vogues in usage, we find it quite believable that a wrought-up farm hand might use personifications like "Labour's rugged school" (1. 8) and "Wherever Nature needs/ Wherever Nature calls" (11. 51–52). Similarly, English farm workers—traditionally known for their simple piety and for the homely appositeness of their biblical allusions—might readily call themselves "Adam's heirs" (1. 75) or refer to the opening verses of Luke 21: "labour's little mite,/ . . . the poor at the temple door" (11. 92–93). The threat of a "New Bastille" would not sound strange on the lips of a desperate British laborer at a time when the French fortress, with its symbolic associations for the oppressed, was still a living memory. Finally, there is one genuine word-play in "The Lay of the Labourer," and it is as properly suited to the speaker's character as is the single pun ("twit") in "The Song of the Shirt": "A-glowing on the haggard cheek,/ And not in the haggard's blaze!" (11. 25–26). ("Haggard" was a fairly common farming term for "hay yard.")

A comparison of "The Lay of the Labourer" and "The Song of the Shirt" shows that both are typical of Hood's practice as a humanitarian poet—a practice that might have been still evolving. It is legitimate to speculate that in their straightforwardness of thought and diction, as in their technical aspects, they show the trend that his work in this genre would have taken had Hood lived longer. Beyond this point, the comparison must not be forced. The poems are quite disparate in tone; that of the "Song" is tragic and pathetic; that of the "Lay," proud and militant. We would scarcely expect identical attitudes from the frail, cowed seamstress in her cell and the hardy, independent laborer in the open field. The rougher tone of the farmer's chant is due largely to the event that prompted the poem, of which there are some explicit echoes in lines 15–26 and 43–50. The quality that comes forward most forcibly in this piece is the speaker's *pride*—pride in his capacity for toil and hardship, pride in his independence, pride in his acceptance of a harsh and lowly existence without the least feeling

of inferiority, pride in his insistence that the laborer is worthy of
his hire:

> No parish money, or loaf,
>   No pauper badges for me,
> A son of the soil, by right of toil
>   Entitled to my fee.
> No alms I ask, give me my task:
>   Here are the arm, the leg,
> The strength, the sinews of a Man,
>   To work, and not to beg.
>   (11. 67–74)

There is pathos here because of the compassion that all must feel
toward the man who can suffer unjustly without losing either his
decency or his self-respect.

"The Lay of the Labourer" is on the whole a vigorous and well-
made poem of social protest. Its chief limitation as poetry is that
of nearly all its kind: polemics almost inevitably have a temporal-
izing and thus a limiting effect. Compared with other works of
its kind, like Shelley's "Song to the Men of England," Hood's poem
holds its own very well.

III *Hood's Last Days*

Hood was more than willing to continue in his role as public
poet, but his strength was practically gone. His newly founded
and thus far successful magazine seemed doomed; and so it would
have been but for the help of devoted friends and colleagues,
some of whom contributed to it gratis and in several cases per-
suaded others to do the same. Consequently, an index to *Hood's
Monthly Magazine* resembles a catalogue of literary luminaries of
the day, among them Robert Browning, Edward Bulwer-Lytton,
Bryan Waller Procter, Walter Savage Landor, and of course
Dickens. Less famous but signally deserving of recognition is the
name of Frederick Oldfield Ward, who served as editor without
pay after Hood's collapse. Some of the poet's more influential
well-wishers rendered him another great kindness in having Mrs.
Hood's name placed on the civil pension list.[62]

Hood seldom left his sickroom after November, 1844, although—
amazingly—he still contributed an occasional bit of writing or a
humorous drawing to his magazine. After the advent of 1845, he

limited his writing mostly to farewell letters, in which, as the following one shows, the Hood wit remained irrepressible:

DEAR MOIR,

God bless you and yours, and good-by! I drop these few lines, as in a bottle from a ship water-logged, and on the brink of foundering, being in the last stage of dropsical debility; but though suffering in body, serene in mind. So without reversing my union-jack, I await my last lurch. Till which, believe me, dear Moir,

Yours most truly,

THOMAS HOOD.[63]

It is remarkable, however, that one of Hood's most famous lyrics was written literally on his deathbed. This was "Stanzas: Farewell Life!", published in *Hood's Monthly Magazine* in February, 1845:

> Farewell, Life! My senses swim;
> And the world is growing dim;
> Thronging shadows cloud the light,
> Like the advent of the night,—
> Colder, colder, colder still
> Upward steals a vapour chill—
> Strong the earthy odour grows—
> I smell the Mould above the Rose!
>
> Welcome, Life! the Spirit strives!
> Strength returns, and hope revives;
> Cloudy fears and shapes forlorn
> Fly like shadows at the morn,—
> O'er the earth there comes a bloom—
> Sunny light for sullen gloom,
> Warm perfume for vapour cold—
> I smell the Rose above the Mould!

These lines reveal the tough and essentially optimistic spirit of a man plucking hope from the open grave itself. No exemplar of institutional, hebdomadal piety (we recall the "Ode to Rae Wilson"), Hood had a quiet faith that sustained him during his last days. These facts should not influence us either to overvalue the poem just quoted or to undervalue it for fear of overvaluing it. Viewed quite apart from the situation that produced the work,

[148]

"Stanzas" holds its own as a good but not really exceptional piece of lyric verse.

Before making our final estimate of Hood's poetry, however, it is surely proper to pause a bit to acknowledge that the creative spirit moved in Hood as long as he had life; that he was sufficiently a true poet to practice his art to the last. Let us even go beyond Hood's career as a poet and listen to a friend's comment upon his life as a whole. "In going through the record of his most pure, modest, honorable life, and living along with him, you come to trust him thoroughly, and feel that here is a most loyal, affectionate, and upright soul, with whom you have been brought into communion. Can we say as much of all lives of all men of letters?" [64]

CHAPTER 7

Conclusion

I N our final assessment of Thomas Hood as a writer, it is enough
to say of his prose that, at its best, it shows versatility and wit,
and sometimes moderate force, without ever approaching great-
ness. As for his poetry—a considerable legacy—first let us frankly
recognize Hood's limitations as a poet, without defending them
on account of his personal misfortunes. Hood is an uneven artist
who is never at his best for long; Henley is quite right in saying
that "The immortal part of Hood might be expressed into a single
tiny volume." [1] We find in him no great depth, and seldom any
great subtlety of thought. His lines achieve no soaring lyricism
and his images no intense, many-layered compression; he seems
incapable of volcanic, engulfing passion. Yet, we might do well at
this point to repeat Saintsbury's admission that "to say this is to
say little more than that he was not Shakespeare." [2]

On the credit side, Hood's accomplishments as a poet command
respect. He is an important humorist whose probable influence
on the Victorians has received scholarly notice,[3] and he is generally reckoned the greatest or at least most fertile punster in the
language. Lacking the splenetic force of such satirists as Swift
and Byron, Hood on a more modest level can be effective enough
and even formidable, as in the "Ode to Rae Wilson." As a poet
of the macabre, he certainly challenges Poe; he can make us feel
"zero at the bone" by calling forth the dark forces behind the veil
of everyday reality, as in "The Haunted House," or by penetrating
the tortured guilty mind, as in "The Dream of Eugene Aram."
Few authors have been as successful in wedding the comic and
the horrible as has Hood in the "pathetic ballads" and "Miss Kilmansegg and Her Precious Leg."

Recent critics have inclined more and more to the position that
Hood's greatest achievement was in the lyric; the writer who in

Conclusion

1944 proclaimed his readiness "to defend against all comers the thesis that among the first score of chosen English lyrics there must be at least one by Tom Hood" [4] could count on some distinguished support in this decade.[5] Probably none of Hood's admirers would claim for his lyrics the quality of incandescent intensity, but for this lack there is sufficient recompense. The best of Hood's lyrics before 1843, while diversified in subject and feeling, characteristically show the qualities of wistful delicacy, restraint, simple language, melodic structure, and the use of memorable conceits. Among the lyrics deserving mention in this group are "Fair Ines," "Ruth," "The Death-bed," "The Season," and "I Remember, I Remember." Delicacy and restraint are naturally less visible in the humanitarian poems of 1843–44, which are frankly tendentious and designed to arouse humane indignation and social concern. "The Bridge of Sighs," however, matches and perhaps surpasses the best of the nonpolemical lyrics, and it does so in spite of several noticeable flaws. "The Song of the Shirt," "The Workhouse Clock," and "The Lay of the Labourer" undeniably have power and are—their genre taken into account—generally free of objectionable excess. They may well be the best poems of their kind ever written.

Possibly our later poets have learned more from Hood than they realize. He made a strong impact on many writers from his time to the end of the century, and some of these must have passed on to their successors what they had consciously or unconsciously absorbed from Hood—his verbal harlequinade, his prosodic innovations, his macabre humor, his social consciousness. For example, it is something of a commonplace to see Robert Browning as a forerunner of the moderns, but it has been well argued that Hood was an important influence not only on Browning but indirectly on later poets, including Gerard Manley Hopkins, W. H. Auden, and Ezra Pound.[6]

It was Hood's fortune to be preceded and followed by several artists whose gifts were richer than his. This does not mean, as Emerson might say, that they wore out poetry or that no poet between Keats and Tennyson is worth reading. Between the lofty ranges of High Romantic and of the greatest Victorian poetry are some lower but challenging ones whose heights and declivities are very much worth exploring. Hood belongs in this region of poetic geography. It has been the purpose of this book to show that our knowledge of nineteenth-century English literature and our appreciation of poetry as a whole can be significantly enriched through a study of the works of Thomas Hood.

Notes and References

Chapter One

1. Jacques Barzun, *Darwin, Marx, Wagner* (New York, 1958), p. 143.

2. William Michael Rossetti, *Lives of Famous Poets* (London, 1878), p. 381; Walter Jerrold, *Thomas Hood: His Life and Times* (London, 1907), p. 190; Hugh Walker, *The Literature of the Victorian Era* (Cambridge, 1913), p. 249.

Chapter Two

1. See *The Works of Thomas Hood* (hereafter cited as *Works*), edited with notes by his son and daughter (London, 1869–73), I, 453–55.

2. *Ibid.*, 457.

3. All quotations from Hood's poetry in this book, with the exception made in note 5 below, are from *The Complete Poetical Works of Thomas Hood* (hereafter cited as *Poetical Works*), edited with notes by Walter Jerrold (London, 1906).

4. *Works*, II, 125. The "Literary Reminiscences" here cited must not be confused with the sonnet of that title.

5. Not in *Poetical Works;* forty-eight lines are quoted, unnumbered, in Jerrold, *Thomas Hood,* pp. 37–38.

6. *Works*, II, 362–63.

7. *Ibid.*, 364.

8. Jerrold, p. 87.

9. *Works*, II, 365. Hood alludes to Cunningham's great stature.

10. *Ibid.*, 374–79. The "gallery" continues for several pages; other figures described are Cary, Procter, and Reynolds.

11. *Ibid.*, 387–90; see also 366–73.

12. *Ibid.*, 365.

13. There might be some question about those in the *London* for June, 1823, since it is not known exactly when Hood left his position.

14. A sixth piece appearing in *Whims and Oddities*, "Remonstratory Ode from the Elephant at Exeter Change," was published in the *London* in June, 1825.

15. On Keats's influence upon Hood, see Federico Olivero, "Hood and Keats," *Modern Language Notes*, XXVIII, 8 (December, 1913), 233–35, and especially Alvin Whitley, "Keats and Hood," *Keats-Shelley Journal*, V (Winter, 1956), 33–47. The opinions on the two poets expressed in the present study were formulated before the author had read these works or any other discussion of the subject.

16. *The Revolt of Islam*, 1. 3176.

17. See, among numerous parallels, *ibid.*, 11. 2564, 2661–62, 3925–26.

18. L1. 530–31; see also 11. 221–22.

19. Keats's "Hymn to Apollo"—also known as "Ode to Apollo," a fact causing it to be confused with another poem by Keats with this title—was first printed in the *Western Messenger*, June 1, 1836.

20. J. C. Reid calls "Fair Ines" "perhaps his most charming lyric"; see *Thomas Hood* (London, 1963), p. 38. Compare Agnes Repplier's comment in *In Pursuit of Laughter* (Boston, 1936), p. 153.

21. The poem meets the test of Keats's own "Axioms": see *The Letters of John Keats*, ed. H. E. Rollins (Cambridge, Mass., 1958), I, 238–39.

22. "To Hope," "Ode to Dr. Kitchener," "To a Critic," "To Celia," "Fare Thee Well," "Midnight" (to be examined in Chapter 4), "On a Sleeping Child," "Sonnet Written in Keats's 'Endymion,'" and "Epigram."

23. See *Works*, IV, 325–26, and Jerrold, pp. 97–98.

24. Note the clever change from a passive to an active infinitive in the legal phrase *Curia advisari vult* ("The court wishes to be advised").

25. See Reid, pp. 35–36, 41–42.

Chapter Three

1. On Hood's relations with Reynolds, at this time his closest friend next to Lamb, see Peter F. Morgan, "John Hamilton Reynolds and Thomas Hood," *Keats-Shelley Journal*, XI (Winter, 1962), 83–95.

2. Later Reynolds seems to have felt that his contribution was somewhat larger; on this point see Reid's sensible explanation (p. 61).

3. See Jerrold, pp. 174–75.

4. This is not the same poem as the one mentioned in note 22 to Chapter 2.

5. Minor variations are sometimes found in the printings of these titles; those given are taken from the table of contents of the *Poetical Works*.

6. Quoted in Tom Hood and Frances Freeling Broderip, *Memorials of Thomas Hood* (hereafter cited as *Memorials*), collected, arranged,

and edited by his daughter and with a preface and notes by his son (Boston, 1861), I, 16–17.

7. *The Letters of Charles Lamb,* edited by Alfred Ainger (London, 1904), II, 136.

8. The Miltonic passage is from "L'Allegro," ll. 139–40.

9. Byron did not, of course, *invent* the kind of rime mentioned here; among his models were Swift and Samuel Butler; but Byron made the practice famous and would have been the most likely inspiration for Hood.

10. See also the preceding and following stanzas.

11. See especially *English Bards,* ll. 201–34; "The Vision of Judgment," LXXXV–CV; *Don Juan,* I, ccv, and III, lxxviii–lxxxvi, xciii, xcvii.

12. "Ode to Richard Martin," ll. 44–46; "The Vision of Judgment," l. 721; *English Bards,* ll. 142–45.

13. On Hood as a punster, see Paul Elmer More, *Shelburne Essays: Seventh Series* (New York, 1910), pp. 49–63; W. E. Henley, *Views and Reviews: Essays in Appreciation* (New York, 1897), pp. 167–68; Reid, pp. 250–53.

14. Compare "Captain Parry," ll. 157–58.

15. *Memorials,* I, 16.

16. An echo of the penultimate line of Dryden's "Alexander's Feast": "He rais'd a mortal to the skies."

17. See *Henry IV, Part I,* V.iv.104.

18. See *Hamlet,* III.iv.102; *Macbeth,* I.iii.48–50; *King Lear,* IV.vi, especially l. 163.

19. Of this number, one ("The Stag-Eyed Lady") was included in Chapter 2 because it was first published during Hood's *London Magazine* "apprenticeship"; another ("The Last Man") will be studied in Chapter 4.

20. It appears that Reynolds contributed some lines to "Sally Brown": see Reid, p. 73.

21. So Edwin P. Whipple calls them in *Essays and Reviews* (Boston, 1893), II, 377; Oliver Elton seems to agree, saying that they "are the perfection of a kind that Hood invented." See *A Survey of English Literature, 1780–1830* (London, 1948), II, 290. Elton's work was first published in 1912.

22. See *Works,* I, 448–57, especially 450–55.

23. "Hood's Whims and Oddities," *Blackwood's Edinburgh Magazine,* XXI, 121 (January, 1827), 45–60.

24. Hood soon resigned this position—for which, indeed, he was not very well qualified.

25. *Works,* V, 107.

26. *Memorials,* I, 20–21.

27. Several of the *London Magazine* poems used later in *The Plea* were glanced at in the preceding chapter; two other works in this volume, "Lycus, the Centaur" (also a *London* piece) and "Ode to Melancholy," will receive attention in Chapter 4.

28. For example, "To some unwasted regions of my brain" (1. 15) is clearly a paraphrase of "In some untrodden region of my mind" ("Ode to Psyche," 1. 51), and "crimson barr'd" (1. 30) is taken verbatim from "Lamia" (I, 50).

29. Repplier, p. 157.

30. John Heath-Stubbs, *The Darkling Plain* (London, 1950), p. 52.

31. Rossetti, p. 369.

32. *Ibid.*, pp. 369–70.

33. George Saintsbury, *Essays in English Literature, 1780–1860* (London, 1895), p. 114.

34. Repplier, p. 157.

35. Laurence Brander, *Thomas Hood* (London, 1963), p. 18.

36. Douglas Bush, *Mythology and the Romantic Tradition in English Poetry* (New York, 1963), pp. 189–92; Reid, p. 82. Bush's study was first published in 1937.

37. Hood, 11. 67–70; Keats, III, 133–36. Compare Shelley: *Prometheus Unbound*, IV, 287–311.

38. This poem first appeared in *Friendship's Offering*, one of the many annuals of the period, in 1826.

39. F. W. Bateson, *Wordsworth: A Re-interpretation* (London, 1960), p. 163.

40. Not to be confused with another lyric in *The Plea* bearing the same title; both must be distinguished from "Ode: Autumn."

41. Reid, p. 95.

42. For a full discussion of Hood as a playwright, see Alvin Whitley, "Thomas Hood as a Dramatist," *University of Texas Studies in English*, XXX (1951), 184–201.

43. The point can, however, be debated: see *ibid.*, 187.

44. Reid, p. 92.

45. Whitley, pp. 197–98.

46. *Ibid.*, p. 200.

47. *Ibid.*, p. 201.

48. Mark Twain, *The Adventures of Huckleberry Finn* (New York, 1948), p. 140.

49. See note 38 to this chapter.

50. Jane Reynolds Hood had in her possession Keats's sonnet "On a [Picture of] Leander," one of several uncollected pieces by Keats left in the hands of the Reynolds family at his death.

51. "On an Infant Dying as Soon as Born," Lamb's poem on the death of the Hoods' first child, was published in *The Gem*.

52. It will be studied fully in Chapter 4.
53. Bush, p. 192.
54. Jerrold, p. 4; Reid, p. 10.
55. See lines 271, 464, 427–28, 275–76 (the mock moral at the end also recalls Burns's poem), 319–20.
56. See lines 13–16, 68, 105–8, 131–32, 151–52, 161–64, 241–44, 287–88, 361–64.
57. The sonnet "To Mrs. Reynolds's Cat," another bit of Keatsiana in the custody of the Reynoldses, was first published in this volume.
58. Jerrold, p. 253; Reid, p. 112.
59. *Works,* VI, 171.
60. *Memorials,* I, 38.
61. Charles MacFarlane, *Reminiscences of a Literary Life* (New York, 1917), p. 106.
62. Other such odes are addressed "To Admiral Lord Gambier, G. C. B." (1833), "To Sir Andrew Agnew, Bart." (1834), "To Dr. Hahnemann" (1837), and "To Messrs. Green, Holland, and Monck Mason" (1837).
63. Several of the works listed will be touched on in later chapters.
64. *Memorials,* I, xl.
65. First published in the *New Monthly Magazine,* September, 1840.
66. V. S. Pritchett, *The Living Novel* (New York, 1947), p. 75.
67. In relation to its length, "Miss Kilmansegg" is rather less pun-laden than most of Hood's humorous poems.
68. Others (still only a fraction of the whole) are in lines 36–40, 174–75, 219–31, 303–9, 500–4, 626–38, 1093–95, and 1845–91.
69. See also lines 1442–1536, 1669–76.
70. See also lines 390–438.
71. The present account gives only a faint picture of the hardships endured by Hood and his family.
72. Hood was to publish in his magazine many poems in the familiar comic vein; but the most memorable, like "The Haunted House" and "The Bridge of Sighs," were to be in the genre of terror or of social protest.

Chapter Four

1. *The Complete Works of Edgar Allan Poe,* edited by James A. Harrison (New York, 1902), XVI, 178.
2. See Samuel C. Chew's remarks on these figures in *A Literary History of England,* edited by Albert C. Baugh (New York, 1948), p. 1252; on the general subject of this paragraph, see also Reid, pp. 259–60, and Heath-Stubbs, p. 51.
3. Poe, p. 177; see also Henley, pp. 168–69.

4. Reid, p. 251.

5. See *Memorials*, I, 23–24, 39–41, 123–24, 131.

6. Whipple, p. 376.

7. *[Sic]*.

8. Whipple, p. 377.

9. Revised 1803.

10. Compare Scrooge's using an extinguisher on the Ghost of Christmas Past in Dickens' *A Christmas Carol*.

11. Poe, an admirer of Hood, might have remembered "The Fall" when he wrote "A Descent into the Maëlstrom" (1841).

12. Heath-Stubbs, p. 53.

13. Chapter 3, Section II. Actually Hood wrote two parodies of "The Ancient Mariner"; the second was "The Captain's Cow," printed in *Hood's Monthly Magazine* in March, 1844.

14. Reid, pp. 74, 243.

15. It is important to note that Hood's was the first of the three poems to be *published*. Shelley's "To Night" (written 1821) first appeared in the *Posthumous Poems*, published by Mrs. Shelley in 1824; Keats's "To Sleep" (written 1819) was first printed in the *Plymouth and Devonport Weekly Journal* for October 11, 1838.

16. "Ode to Melancholy" also contains echoes of *Endymion*, "Ode to a Nightingale," and Shelley's *Adonais*.

17. See Chapter 3, Section III.

18. Or, to be technically exact, 113 couplets with a triplet in lines 53–55—429 lines in all.

19. *Poetical Works*, p. 161.

20. Brander's remark (p. 18) that Hood has invented a myth could be misleading. Unquestionably there is some inventiveness in the poem, but Hood's making Lycus a Centaur is not original.

21. There are also some suggestions of "Lamia," as in lines 268–76.

22. See also line 120. Heath-Stubbs mentions some other Dantean features of the poem (p. 57).

23. See Jerrold, p. 197.

24. Rossetti, p. 367.

25. Heath-Stubbs, p. 56.

26. *Ibid.*, pp. 57–58. See Reid's comment, p. 86.

27. Saintsbury, p. 113.

28. First offered in *The Gem*, the poem was issued separately two years later.

29. Readers interested in the details of the charges against Aram should see the account in *The Dictionary of National Biography*, edited by Leslie Stephen and Sidney Lee (London, 1908), I, 525–27.

30. See Hood's Preface to the 1831 publication of the poem in *Works*, VI, 437–38.

31. In "Ode on a Distant Prospect of Clapham Academy." See Chapter 2, Section II.

32. If the surmise that the boy was reading Gessner's story is correct, there is a pardonable anachronism in Hood's poem (unless his youthful reader knew German), since the English translation of *Der Tod Abels* (1758) appeared in 1761, two years after Aram's execution.

33. See *Poetical Works*, p. 211, note, and *Works*, VI, 438.

34. See, for example, lines 351–52, 467–68, 475–76.

35. The best-known of these—"Stanzas: Farewell, Life!"—has been reserved for mention in the conclusion to this book.

36. Introduction to *The Castle of Otranto*, in *The Castle of Otranto, Vathek, The Vampyre: Three Gothic Novels*, edited by E. F. Bleiler (New York, 1966), p. 8.

37. We think at once of "Eugene Aram": "And drew my midnight curtains round/ With fingers bloody red!" (ll. 143–44).

38. See lines 41–68.

39. Italics added.

40. The "Castle of the Body" motif was popular in European literature from the thirteenth through the seventeenth centuries, but the concept is not so obscure that any imaginative mind could not hit on it independently.

41. The opening line of Byron's "Darkness" is "I had a dream, which was not all a dream." Incidentally, an interesting comparison could be made between "Darkness" and Hood's "The Sea of Death: A Fragment."

Chapter Five

1. Because of the hectic nature of Hood's journalistic career, it is sometimes difficult to determine whether or not a given minor work came from his hand. Hood's son and daughter were commendably industrious and conscientious in collecting his works; but they were not trained scholars, and some of the pieces included in the *Works* are suspect. Such works are not considered in this study.

2. This piece should be compared with the later "Sketches on the Road," which are scattered through volumes I, II, III, IV, and VI of the *Works*.

3. *Works*, IV, 357–58. Strong echoes of Sterne are heard in many of Hood's writings, and two—"A Friend in Need: An Extravaganza after Sterne" and "English Retrogression"—are dominated by him.

4. *Ibid.*, 361–65.

5. *Ibid.*, 365–67.

6. *Ibid.*, 367–68.

7. *Ibid.*, 368–71.

8. Chapter 2, Sections I and II.
9. For example, see Elton, p. 291.
10. *Works,* II, 13.
11. *Works,* III, 170–71.
12. *Ibid.,* 173.
13. *Ibid.,* 233.
14. *Ibid.,* 234.
15. *Ibid.,* 255–56.
16. *Ibid.,* 272. For Hood's views, see (among other places) *Memorials,* I, 137–73, *passim.*
17. *Works,* III, 273–74.
18. *Ibid.,* 278.
19. See *Works,* I, 448–57.
20. *Works,* III, 305.
21. *Works,* IV, 62–63.
22. *Ibid.,* 70–73.
23. *Ibid.,* 76–77.
24. Serjeant-at-Law, a barrister of the highest rank.
25. It deserves to be recorded that William Wordsworth, who many believe lost all interest in reform as his poetic light grew dim, petitioned the House of Commons in support of Talfourd's bill in May, 1839. Wordsworth was then sixty-nine.
26. *Works,* VI, 380–81.
27. *Works,* I, 226.
28. *Ibid.,* 228.
29. *Whimsicalities,* in which the last two stories appeared, was dated 1844 although published late in 1843. Both stories had been printed earlier in the *New Monthly Magazine.*
30. *Works,* III, 364.
31. See the note on this story by Hood's son in *The Works of Thomas Hood,* edited wtih notes by his son (London, 1862–63), V, 382. Hereafter this edition will be cited as *Works* (1862) to distinguish it from the edition of 1869–73.
32. *Works,* IX, 94.
33. See Reid, p. 180.
34. *Works,* (1862), V, 356.
35. *Ibid.,* 357.
36. *Ibid.,* 358–59.
37. *Ibid.,* 361.
38. *Works,* V, 107. See Chapter 3, Section II.
39. Several matters in "The Two Faithful Lovers of Sicily" strongly suggest Heliodorus' *Aethiopica;* the island episode recalls Longus' "Daphnis and Chloë."

40. See "The Lady in Love with Romance" and especially "The German Knight."

41. For example, "The Eighth Sleeper of Ephesus" and "The Miracle of the Holy Hermit."

42. Such as the miserly Malatesti and "the noted robber Pazzo" in "The Florentine Kinsmen" and Alfieri in "Geronimo and Ghisola."

43. Rossetti, p. 369.

44. *Works,* VI, 56–57.

45. *Works,* V, 320–22.

46. *Ibid.,* 320.

47. Jerrold, p. 223.

48. *Ibid.,* p. 221.

49. *Ibid.*

50. Saintsbury, p. 116.

51. More, p. 51.

52. Brander, p. 25.

53. Reid, p. 76.

54. It is worth noting that this is the only one specifically mentioned by Reid and that his reference is comparatively favorable (*ibid.*).

55. Most critics seem to consider *Tylney Hall* Hood's only novel; the question turns on whether or not *Up the Rhine* and the fragmentary *Our Family* should be counted as novels.

56. See Reid, p. 123.

57. Quoted by Jerrold, p. 272; Reid, pp. 122–23.

58. *Works* (1862), III, 23.

59. Possibly this refers to the hostile review in *Fraser's Magazine,* which ridiculed not only Hood's novel but the person to whom it was dedicated, the Duke of Devonshire.

60. See Saintsbury, p. 111; Henley, p. 167; Jerrold, pp. 272–75; Brander, pp. 25–26; Reid, pp. 122–24.

61. Since in 1834 Hood was living at Lake House, once a part of the Tylney estates, it is a natural assumption that the history of the Tylneys supplied some of the matter for *Tylney Hall.* This was, however, denied by Hood: see *Works* (1862), III, 22–23.

62. *Ibid.,* 326–28.

63. *Ibid.,* 414–15.

64. *Works* (1862), IV, 62.

65. *Works* (1862), III, 423–28.

66. Unfortunately, even this device is partially spoiled by Hood's unwillingness to leave well enough alone: the revelation at the end of Chapter XXXIV that the "stranger" is Marguerite in disguise is crudely melodramatic as well as practically incredible, and her speech on conscience just prior to this seems quite out of character.

67. *Works* (1862), III, 422.
68. See *ibid.*, 177–78, 183; 383–89, 437–38; IV, 18–22.
69. *Works* (1862), IV, 17.
70. *King Lear*, I.ii.1–22.
71. Both Jerrold (p. 273) and Reid (p. 124) stress the fact that some of Hood's characterizations anticipated those of Dickens.
72. *Works* (1862), III, 263.
73. See *ibid.*, 42–43, 247–52.
74. *Ibid.*, 25; IV, 117.
75. See Brander, p. 26.
76. See *ibid.* and Reid, p. 124.
77. *Works* (1862), III, 166–68.
78. *Ibid.*, 272–73.
79. *Works* (1862), IV, 76–86.
80. See especially *ibid.*, 82.
81. *Ibid.*, 54–56.
82. *Works* (1862), III, 367–69.
83. *Works* (1862), IV, 37–47.
84. *Works* (1862), III, 325–58.
85. *Ibid.*, 416–19.
86. Published at the end of 1839; dated 1840.
87. In his Preface to the second edition, *Works*, VII, 2.
88. An exception is Émile Legouis and Louis Cazamian, *A History of English Literature* (New York, 1957), which has a three-line comment on the work (p. 291). This book was first published in 1926–27.
89. Saintsbury, pp. 111, 117.
90. Reid, pp. 172–73.
91. Preface to the first edition, *Works*, VII, 1.
92. *Ibid.*, p. 56.
93. Richard Orchard also writes one letter to Dr. Truby.
94. See *Works*, VII, 68, 73, 82, 95.
95. *Ibid.*, 93.
96. *Ibid.*, 95.
97. *Ibid.*, 101–2.
98. *Ibid.*, 123. Among other incidents related from several viewpoints should be noted the mixup in the customs (pp. 60–63, 67–68, 88) and Martha's interception on her way to mass (pp. 167–68, 174–75, 181–82).
99. *Ibid.*, 226, 228, 183–87.
100. *Ibid.*, 22.
101. *Ibid.*, 24.
102. *Ibid.*, 87.
103. *Ibid.*, 107.
104. *Ibid.*, 134.

105. *Ibid.*, 42.
106. *Ibid.*, 159. This incident, like several others in the book, is taken directly from the Hoods' experience in Germany; see *Memorials,* I, 77–78.
107. *Works,* VII, 209.
108. *Ibid.*, 138–39.
109. *Ibid.*, 151.
110. *Ibid.*, 201–2.
111. *Ibid.*, 134–35.
112. In the story "A Simple Heart" ("Un Coeur Simple").
113. *Works,* IX, 299–303.
114. *Ibid.*, 290–93, 304–10.
115. *Ibid.*, 321–29.
116. Brander, pp. 26–27.

Chapter Six

1. Reid, pp. 258 ff.
2. *Ibid.*, pp. 262–64.
3. The "Answer" was made to the author of "Reply to a Pastoral Poet," signed "Pauper," which had appeared in an earlier issue of the magazine.
4. Chapter 3, Section V.
5. See lines 121–22, 168 of the poem and note in *Poetical Works,* pp. 468–69.
6. *Poetical Works,* pp. 760–61.
7. See especially the first, fourth, and fifth stanzas.
8. See Chapter 5, Section I.
9. *Works,* VII, 318–22.
10. "A Plain Direction," one of the better poems in this list, received a brief comment in Chapter 3, Section V.
11. See especially lines 1–8, 29–36.
12. Shakespeare, *A Midsummer Night's Dream,* I.ii.84–85.
13. For example: Blake, "London," 11. 11–12; Wordsworth, *The Prelude,* IV, 387–469; Coleridge, "Religious Musings," 11. 293–300.
14. See *Poetical Works,* p. 752, note.
15. See Chapter 3, Section V.
16. Sigmund Freud, *A General Introduction to Psychoanalysis* (Garden City, 1938), pp. 327–28. The lectures comprised by this work were first published in 1916–17; an English translation followed in 1920.
17. Walker, p. 251.
18. Jerrold, p. 368. It seems a pity that Hood did not wait about a month and publish the poem in the first issue of his own magazine.
19. See Reid, pp. 207–8; Jerrold, pp. 365–66.

20. *Memorials,* II, 165–66.

21. See Reid, pp. 208–9.

22. An iamb followed by two monosyllabic feet is used in two of the twelve occurrences of the refrain, one in the second stanza and the other in the eighth.

23. The fifth, ninth, and tenth.

24. Stanza eleven was not included in the first publication of the poem; see *Poetical Works,* p. 626. Many readers consider its addition unfortunate.

25. The second, third, sixth, seventh, and eighth. The refrain words are variously punctuated.

26. It is used in only the first line of stanza six.

27. The first, fourth, and twelfth.

28. Chapter 2, Section II.

29. Stanza twelve has "sate" instead of "sat" in the third line and "this" instead of "the" in the last.

30. In Wordsworth's Preface to the second edition of *Lyrical Ballads* (1800). See *The Poetical Works of Wordsworth,* edited by Thomas Hutchinson (London, 1960), p. 735.

31. *The Letters of John Keats,* II , 80.

32. "Lycidas," 1. 119.

33. Alexander Pope, *An Essay on Criticism,* 11. 253–54.

34. See note 24 to this chapter.

35. Under public pressure, the authorities changed the woman's sentence to a prison term of seven years.

36. Jerrold, p. 379.

37. William Makepeace Thackeray, *Roundabout Papers* (New York, 1863), p. 116.

38. Saintsbury, p. 114.

39. *Ibid.,* p. 120.

40. *Ibid.,* p. 121.

41. Saintsbury's remarks on "The Bridge of Sighs" were first published in 1890, Walker's and Elton's in 1910 and 1912, respectively.

42. Walker, p. 252.

43. Elton, p. 290.

44. Chew, p. 1254.

45. Pritchett, p. 76.

46. *Samson Agonistes,* 11. 668–69.

47. Brander, p. 39.

48. Reid, pp. 215–17.

49. Alexander Pope, *Epistle to Dr. Arbuthnot,* 1. 308.

50. Note the use of consonance, seen also in lines 17 and 20, 36–37, 60–61.

51. See Virgil, *Aeneid,* I, 462.

52. See Chapter 2, Section II.
53. *Memorials*, II, 212.
54. *Works*, IX, 238.
55. *Ibid.*, 244–45.
56. *Memorials*, II, 212.
57. *Works*, IX, 247.
58. *Memorials*, II, 213.
59. *Ibid.*, 222.
60. Chew, for one, thinks that Hood's works were as important as Dickens' in stimulating reform (p. 1254); in this connection, see Reid's comment, p. 217.
61. Except in the long third stanza of the "Lay," which rhymes *abcbdedefe,* a kind of blend of the two schemes. Note the similar placement of the *abcbdefe* pattern in the two poems—in stanzas 4, 6, 9, 10, 11 of the "Song" and in 4, 6, 7, 8, 9, 10 of the "Lay."
62. See *Memorials*, II, 217–24.
63. *Ibid.*, 232.
64. Thackeray, p. 122.

Chapter Seven

1. Henley, p. 166.
2. Saintsbury, p. 121.
3. See Heath-Stubbs, p. 51; Reid, pp. 259–60.
4. "Quintus Quiz," "Tom Hood," *The Christian Century*, XVI, 4 (August 23, 1944), 968.
5. See Brander, p. 15, and especially Reid, p. 89.
6. See Reid, pp. 261–62; J. M. Cohen, "Thomas Hood: The Language of Poetry," *Times Literary Supplement*, 19 Sept. 1952, pp. 605–6.

Selected Bibliography

PRIMARY SOURCES

HOOD, THOMAS. *The Complete Poetical Works of Thomas Hood*, edited, with notes by Walter Jerrold. London: Oxford University Press, 1906. The standard edition of Hood's poems, and the only reliable one; unfortunately out of print.

————. *The Complete Works of Thomas Hood*, edited, with notes, by his son and daughter. London: Edward Moxon, Son, and Company, 1882–84.

————. *The Works of Thomas Hood*, edited, with notes, by his son. London: Edward Moxon and Company, 1862–63.

————. *The Works of Thomas Hood*, edited, with notes, by his son and daughter. London: Edward Moxon, Son, and Company, 1869–73.

MARCHAND, LESLIE A. (ed.). *Letters of Thomas Hood from the Dilke Papers in the British Museum.* New Brunswick: *Rutgers University Studies in English*, No. 4, 1951. Gives, with commentary, the text of sixteen previously unpublished letters by Hood and five pages of "Miscellaneous—Poetry and Prose."

WHITLEY, ALVIN. "Hood and Dickens: Some New Letters," *Huntingdon Library Quarterly*, XVI, 4 (August, 1951), 385–413. Gives, with commentary, the full text of twenty previously unpublished letters from Hood to Dickens.

SECONDARY SOURCES

Only the most important items are listed; others are mentioned in "Notes and References."

1. *Chiefly Biographical*

HOOD, TOM, AND FRANCIS FREELING BRODERIP. *Memorials of Thomas Hood.* London: Edward Moxon and Company, 1860. A labor of love rather than of scholarship, but an invaluable source for material on Hood's life. Includes a number of his letters.

————. *Memorials of Thomas Hood.* Collected, arranged, and edited by his daughter, with a preface and notes by his son. Boston: Ticknor and Fields, 1861. American edition of the preceding work.

JERROLD, WALTER. *Thomas Hood: His Life and Times.* London: Alston Rivers, 1907. Very valuable source. Contains many quotations from letters and reminiscences (both Hood's and others') which give the work life and authenticity. Attempts comparatively little criticism, but some of it is still helpful. Has a few errors, which later scholarship (e.g., Reid's) has corrected.

LANE, WILLIAM G. "A Chord in Melancholy: Hood's Last Years," *Keats-Shelley Journal,* XIII (Winter, 1964), 43–60. Well-organized, thoroughly documented account, relying mainly on letters by, to, or about Hood; includes eight Hood letters hitherto unpublished.

2. *Biographical and Critical*

BRANDER, LAURENCE. *Thomas Hood. Writers and Their Work,* No. 159. London: Longmans, Green and Company, 1963. Compact and lucidly written; good introduction to the life and work of Hood.

CLUBBE, JOHN. *Victorian Forerunner: The Later Career of Thomas Hood.* Durham, N.C.: Duke University Press, 1968. Important contribution to Hood scholarship that appeared too late to be used in this study. Clubbe is editor of the attractive and useful *Selected Poems of Thomas Hood* (Cambridge, Mass.: Harvard University Press, 1970).

REID, J. C. *Thomas Hood.* London: Routledge and Kegan Paul, 1963. First full-length biographical and critical study of Hood to appear since Jerrold's. Sympathetic but judicious; carefully researched, penetrating, and well written.

3. *Critical: General Studies*

AINGER, ALFRED. Preface to *Humorous Poems.* London: Macmillan and Company, 1893. Fine appreciation, with special attention to Hood's genius as a punster.

BLUNDEN, EDMUND. "The Poet Hood," *Review of English Literature,* I, 1 (January, 1960), 26–34. Good survey of Hood's poetic career.

BUSH, DOUGLAS. "Thomas Hood," in *Mythology and the Romantic Tradition in English Poetry.* New York: W. W. Norton and Company, 1963. Just and perceptive brief coverage; especially valuable for its material on "Lycus, the Centaur" and "Hero and Leander."

CHEW, SAMUEL C. "Thomas Hood, Thomas Lovell Beddoes, and

Other Poets." *A Literary History of England.* Edited by Albert C. Baugh. New York: Appleton-Century-Crofts, 1948. Best account of Hood and his contemporaries to be found in a literary history.

EDEN, HELEN P. "Thomas Hood," *The Catholic World,* CXXIII, 738 (September, 1926), 731–38. Well-written critical sketch of Hood; would serve admirably as an introduction to the man and his work.

HEATH-STUBBS, JOHN. *The Darkling Plain.* London: Eyre and Spottiswoode, 1950. Penetrating book. Estimate of Hood's poetry blends sympathy and sternness; tends to overstress its symbolic and mythic qualities (pp. 22–24, 49–59).

HENLEY, W. E. "Hood." *Views and Reviews: Essays in Appreciation.* New York: Charles Scribner's Sons, 1897. Both sympathetic and discerning; stresses the duality in Hood's career.

MASSON, DAVID. "Thomas Hood," *Macmillan's Magazine,* II (August, 1860), 315–24. Written eleven decades ago, this remains one of the sanest, most comprehensive, and most gracefully written short studies of Hood and his poetry.

MORE, PAUL ELMER. "Thomas Hood." *Shelburne Essays: Seventh Series.* New York: G. P. Putnam's Sons, 1910. Challenges the image of Hood as an unfulfilled serious poet; believes that Hood's fame rests on his role as "the inimitable equivocator in words."

PRITCHETT, V. S. "Our Half-Hogarth." *The Living Novel.* New York: Reynal and Hitchcock, 1947. Excellent essay on Hood's wit and humor.

REPPLIER, AGNES. "The Price of Laughter." *In Pursuit of Laughter.* Boston: Houghton Mifflin Company, 1936. Sensitive, judicious presentation of the thesis that "the quality of a few stray poems" shows how much Hood's "pursuit of laughter" cost him and his readers.

ROSSETTI, WILLIAM MICHAEL. "Thomas Hood." *Lives of Famous Poets.* London: Edward Moxon, Son, and Company, 1878. Sees Hood as "the first English poet between the generation of Shelley and the generation of Tennyson."

SAINTSBURY, GEORGE. "Thomas Hood." *Essays in English Literature 1780–1860.* Second Series. London: J. M. Dent and Company, 1895. Considers Hood's chief distinction to rest on his combining of the serious and comic veins in poetry.

WALKER, HUGH. *The Literature of the Victorian Era.* Cambridge: Cambridge University Press, 1913. Shares Rossetti's estimate of the place of Hood in nineteenth-century English poetry.

4. Critical: Special Studies

GILMAN, MARGARET. "Baudelaire and Thomas Hood," *Romanic Review*, XXVI, 3 (July-September, 1935), 240–44. On Baudelaire's translation of a passage from *Whims and Oddities* and its relationship to his *Salon de 1859* and the earlier *De la Caricature*.

HENNIG, JOHN. "The Literary Relations between Goethe and Thomas Hood," *Modern Language Quarterly*, XII, 1 (March, 1951), 57–66. Survey's Goethe's review of *Whims and Oddities*, discusses Hood's references to Goethe, and argues—not very convincingly—that "The Bridge of Sighs" derives from *Faust*.

MORGAN, PETER F. "John Hamilton Reynolds and Thomas Hood," *Keats-Shelley Journal*, XI (Winter, 1962), 83–95. Carefully documented account of the relationship betwen the two men.

OLIVERO, FEDERICO. "Hood and Keats," *Modern Language Notes*, XXVIII, 8 (December, 1913), 233–35. On Hood's debt to Keats; chiefly parallels.

WHITLEY, ALVIN. "Keats and Hood," *Keats-Shelley Journal*, V (Winter, 1956), 33–47. Part I surveys Hood's relations with the "Keats Circle," particularly the Reynoldses; Part II examines the Keatsian elements in Hood's poetry. A valuable article.

——. "Thomas Hood as a Dramatist," *The University of Texas Studies in English*, XXX (1951), 184–201. The only extended treatment of the subject. Clear, thorough, and sensible as to the conclusions drawn.

Index

Index

154; "Faithless Nelly Gray," 47, 66; "Faithless Sally Brown," 47, 66, 155; "The Fall," 73; "The Fall of the Deer," 47; "Fare Thee Well," 154; "The Farewell," 55; "A Few Lines on Completing Forty-Seven," 75; "The Forge," 72; "Fragment: Probably Written During Illness," 75; "A Friendly Address to Mrs. Fry," 35, 36, 38, 40, 42–43, 44, 121; "The Green Man," 69; "The Haunted House," 66, 67, 72, 76, 79, 85, 86, 88–93, 150, 157; "Hero and Leander," 52–53, 56; "Hit or Miss," 59; "To Hope," 154; "Hymn to the Sun," 27–28; "I'm Not a Single Man," 58; "I Remember, I Remember," Preface, 53, 54, 151; "The Irish Schoolmaster," 48; "John Day," 69; "The Lady's Dream," 19, 135, 136–37, 139; "A Lament for the Decline of Chivalry," 69; "The Lament of Toby," 69; "The Lark and the Rook," 125, 126; "The Last Man," 73–75, 80, 136, 155; "Laying Down the Law," 125, 126; "The Lay of the Labourer," 19, 122, 136, 144–47, 151, 165; "Lines on the Celebration of Peace," 125–26; "Literary Reminiscences," 21; "Lycus, the Centaur," 77–79, 156, 158; "Mary's Ghost," 54, 69; "The Mermaid of Margate," 48; "Midnight," 76, 154; "Miss Kilmansegg and Her Precious Leg," 18, 61 ff., 66, 67, 150; "Ode: Autumn," 31–33, 156; "Ode for St. Cecilia's Eve," 60; "Ode: Imitated from Horace," 122; "Ode on a Distant Prospect of Clapham Academy," 33, 159; "Ode to Captain Parry," 35, 36, 37, 40, 43, 155; "Ode to Dr. Hahnemann," 69, 157; "Ode to Dr. Kitchener," 154; "Ode to H. Bodkin," 35, 36, 37, 69, 121; "Ode to Joseph Grimaldi," 35, 36, 37, 44; "Ode to Joseph Hume,"

58; "Ode to J. S. Buckingham," 122–23; "Ode to Melancholy," 76, 85, 156, 158; "Ode to Mr. Graham," 35, 36, 37, 40–41, 44; "Ode to Mr. Malthus," 69, 71–72; "Ode to Rae Wilson," 60–61, 122, 148, 150; "Ode to Richard Martin," 35, 36, 37–38, 39, 41, 43, 121, 155; "Ode to Sir Andrew Agnew," 122, 157; "Ode to Spencer Perceval," 69; "Ode to the Cameleopard," 54; "Ode to the Great Unknown," 35, 36, 37, 40, 41, 43; "Ode to W. Kitchener," 35, 36, 37, 39, 43; "On a Picture of Hero and Leander," 55; "On a Sleeping Child," 154; "On Lieutenant Eyre's Narrative," 64; "On the Death of Sir Walter Scott," 59; "An Open Question," 59; "Party Spirit," 125; "The Pauper's Christmas Carol," 135; "A Plain Direction," 59, 125, 135, 163; "The Plea of the Midsummer Fairies," 50–52; "The Poacher," 69; "Pompey's Ghost," 71; "The Progress of Art," 54; "A Public Dinner," 58; "The Quakers' Conversazione," 125; "A Reflection on New Year's Eve," 125; "Remonstratory Ode," 47, 153; "A Retrospective Review," 53; "Ruth," 53, 151; "Sally Simpkin's Lament," 69, 70, 71; "The Sausage-Maker's Ghost," 69; "The Sea of Death," 159; "The Season," 64, 151; "The Sea-Spell," 48, 74, 80, 136; "The Song of the Shirt," Preface, 18, 19, 63, 122, 123, 127–35, 136, 137, 139, 140, 143, 145, 146, 151, 165; "Song: The stars are with the voyager,'" 53; "Sonnet Written in Keats's 'Endymion,'" 154; "The Stag-Eyed Lady," 25, 155; "Stanzas: Farewell Life!" 148–49; 159; "Stanzas: Is there a bitter pang," 87–88; "The Supper Superstition," 70; "The Sweep's Complaint," 123–24; "Symptoms of Ossifica-

Hood, Thomas, *Poems* (*cont.*)
tion," 75; "A Tale of a Trumpet,"
59; "To a Cold Beauty," 27; "To
a Critic," 154; "To Admiral Lord
Gambier," 157; "To an Absentee,"
27; "To an Enthusiast," 26; "To
Fancy," 26; "To Messrs. Green,
Holland, and Monck Mason," 157;
"To Silence," 26–27; "A True
Story," 69; "The Two Peacocks of
Bedfont," 30; "The Two Swans,"
33; "The University Feud," 125;
"Verses Mistaken for an Incen-
diary Song," 125; "The Vision," 58;
'A Winter Nosegay," 47; "The
Workhouse Clock," 19, 135, 137–
39, 151
Prose: "The Apparition," 101;
"The Black and White Question,"
100–101, 124; "The Chestnut
Tree," 105; "Copyright and Copy-
wrong," 99–100; "The Eighth
Sleeper of Ephesus," 105, 161;
English Retrogression," 159; "The
Fair Maid of Ludgate," 105–6;
"Fishing in Germany," 97; "The
Florentine Kinsmen," 161; "A
Friend in Need," 159; "The Ger-
man Knight," 161; "Geronimo and
Ghisola," 161; "The Grimsby
Ghost," 101; "The Happiest Man
in England," 98–99; "Johnson-
iana," 96; "The Lady in Love
with Romance," 161; "Literary
Reminiscences," 22, 24, 95–96,
98, 153; "The Miracle of the Holy
Hermit," 105, 161; *National Tales,*
49, 101, 104–6, 118; *Our Family,*
104, 113, 118–20, 161; "The
Owl," 105; "Queries in Natural
History," 96; "The Schoolmistress
Abroad," 97–98; "A Sentimental
Journey from Islington to Water-
loo Bridge," 33–34, 94–95;
"Sketches on the Road," 159;
"The Spanish Tragedy," 105;
"Speculations of a Naturalist,"
96–97; "The Story of Michel Ar-
genti," 105; "A Tale of Terror,"

101; "A Tale of the Great Plague,"
101; "The Two Faithful Lovers of
Sicily," 160; *Tylney Hall,* 58, 104,
106–13, 114, 118, 120, 161; "The
Undertaker," 99; *Up the Rhine,*
104, 109, 113–18, 120, 161
Plays: "Lamia: a Romance," 54;
"Lost and Found.—A Fragment,"
55; *York and Lancaster,* 55
*Collections, Periodicals: Comic
Annuals,* 21, 57 ff., 64, 65, 94, 96,
106, 108, 125; *Hood's Monthly
Magazine,* 65, 88, 94, 102, 135,
144, 147, 148, 158; *Hood's Own,*
64, 94, 125; *Odes and Addresses
to Great People,* 35 ff., 54, 121;
*The Plea of the Midsummer
Fairies . . . and Other Poems,* 25,
30, 49 ff., 76–77, 105, 156; *Whims
and Oddities, First Series,* 25, 46–
48, 74; *Whims and Oddities,
Second Series,* 48–49, 54; *Whim-
sicalities,* 64, 94, 125, 160
Hood, Tom (Hood's son), 57, 105,
129, 153, 154, 159, 160, 167
Hopkins, Gerard Manley, 151
Horace, 27, 30, 103
Hugo, Victor, 15
Hume, David, 44
Hunt, Leigh, 30, 36, 51, 142

James, Henry, 90
Jeffrey, Francis, 41
Jerrold, Walter, Preface, 105, 114,
140, 153, 154, 157, 158, 161, 162,
163, 164, 167, 168
Johnson, Samuel, 15, 51, 96, 97
Juvenal, 41–42

Keats, John, 15, 16, 18, 26, 27, 28,
30, 31–32, 49, 50, 51, 52–53, 54,
55, 57, 76–77, 85, 88, 92, 132,
151, 154, 156, 158

Lamb, Charles, 23–25, 36, 48, 49,
50, 55, 95, 98, 99, 106–7, 110,
112, 155, 156
Lamb, Mary, 49
Landor, Walter Savage, 25, 147

Index

Thackeray, William Makepeace, 66, 140, 164, 165
Theophrastus, 99
Thomas, Dylan, 15
Thomson, James, 30
Thurber, James, 19
The Times, 128, 129
Twain, Mark, 55, 115, 156

Virgil, 164

Walker, Hugh, 20, 127, 141, 153, 163, 164, 169
Walpole, Horace, 88

Ward, Frederick Oldfield, 147
Watts, Isaac, 44
Waugh, Evelyn, 99
White, Gifford, 19, 144–45
Whipple, Edwin P., 155, 158
Whitley, Alvin, 55, 154, 156, 167, 170
William IV, 57
Wordsworth, William, 23, 29, 30, 44, 51, 53, 92, 125, 131, 137, 160, 163, 164
Wren, Sir Christopher, 44

Young, Edward, 44